function	keyboard command	function	keyboard command
Lesson 7		Double open quotation mark	
Maximize a window	Ctrl+F10	Double und word	
Minimize a window	Alt+F9	Ellipsis	
Move a window	Ctrl+F7, Arrow Keys, Enter	Enlarge the font by 1 point	Ctrl+]
New document	Ctrl+N	Enlarge the font one size	Ctrl+Shift+>
Next document window	Ctrl+F6	Font	Ctrl+D
Next pane	F6	Hidden text	Ctrl+Shift+H
Previous document window	Ctrl+Shift+F6	Increase kerning	Ctrl+Shift+]
Previous pane	Shift+F6	Italic	Ctrl+I
Restore a document window	Ctrl+F5	Plain text	Ctrl+Shift+Z
Size a document window	Ctrl+F8	Reduce the font by 1 point	Ctrl+[
Split window	Alt+Ctrl+S	Reduce the font one size	Ctrl+Shift+<
Lesson 8		Registered trademark symbol	Alt+Ctrl+R
All capital letters	Ctrl+Shift+A	Single closing quotation mark	Ctrl+','
Bold	Ctrl+B	Single opening quotation mark	Ctrl+','
Change case	Shift+F3	Small capital letters	Ctrl+Shift+K
Change font size with the Toolbar	Ctrl+Shift+P	Subscripts	Ctrl+=
Change the font with the Toolbar	Ctrl+Shift+F	Superscript	Ctrl+Shift+=
Copyright symbol	Alt+Ctrl+C	Symbol font	Ctrl+Shift+Q
Decrease kerning	Ctrl+Shift+[	Trademark symbol	Alt+Ctrl+T
Double closing quotation mark	Ctrl+","	Underline	Ctrl+U
		Underline a word	Ctrl+Shift+W

For every kind of computer user, there is a SYBEX book.

All computer users learn in their own way. Some need straightforward and methodical explanations. Others are just too busy for this approach. But no matter what camp you fall into, SYBEX has a book that can help you get the most out of your computer and computer software while learning at your own pace.

Beginners generally want to start at the beginning. The **ABC's** series, with its step-by-step lessons in plain language, helps you build basic skills quickly. Or you might try our **Quick & Easy** series, the friendly, full-color guide.

The **Mastering** and **Understanding** series will tell you everything you need to know about a subject. They're perfect for intermediate and advanced computer users, yet they don't make the mistake of leaving beginners behind.

If you're a busy person and are already comfortable with computers, you can choose from two SYBEX series—**Up & Running** and **Running Start**. The **Up & Running** series gets you started in just 20 lessons. Or you can get two books in one, a step-by-step tutorial and an alphabetical reference, with our **Running Start** series.

Everyone who uses computer software can also use a computer software reference. SYBEX offers the gamut—from portable **Instant References** to comprehensive **Encyclopedias, Desktop References**, and **Bibles**.

SYBEX even offers special titles on subjects that don't neatly fit a category—like **Tips & Tricks**, the **Shareware Treasure Chests**, and a wide range of books for Macintosh computers and software.

SYBEX books are written by authors who are expert in their subjects. In fact, many make their living as professionals, consultants or teachers in the field of computer software. And their manuscripts are thoroughly reviewed by our technical and editorial staff for accuracy and ease-of-use.

So when you want answers about computers or any popular software package, just help yourself to SYBEX.

For a complete catalog of our publications, please write:

SYBEX Inc.
2021 Challenger Drive
Alameda, CA 94501
Tel: (510) 523-8233/(800) 227-2346 Telex: 336311
Fax: (510) 523-2373

SYBEX is committed to using natural resources wisely to preserve and improve our environment. As a leader in the computer book publishing industry, we are aware that over 40% of America's solid waste is paper. This is why we have been printing the text of books like this one on recycled paper since 1982.

This year our use of recycled paper will result in the saving of more than 15,300 trees. We will lower air pollution effluents by 54,000 pounds, save 6,300,000 gallons of water, and reduce landfill by 2,700 cubic yards.

In choosing a SYBEX book you are not only making a choice for the best in skills and information, you are also choosing to enhance the quality of life for all of us.

The ABCs
of Word 6
for Windows

The ABCs of
Word 6
for
Windows™

Alan R. Neibauer

SYBEX ®

San Francisco   Paris   Düsseldorf   Soest

Coordinating Editor: Joanne Cuthbertson
Developmental Editor: Sarah Wadsworth
Editor: Armin Brott
Project Editor: Valerie Potter
Technical Editor: Horace Shelton
Book Designer and Artist: Ingrid Owen
Screen Graphics: Cuong Le and Aldo Bermudez
Typesetter: Alissa Feinberg
Production Coordinator: David Silva
Indexer: Nancy Guenther
Cover Designer: Archer Design
Cover Illustrator: Richard Miller

Screen reproductions produced with Collage Plus.

Collage Plus is a trademark of Inner Media Inc.

SYBEX is a registered trademark of SYBEX Inc.

TRADEMARKS: SYBEX has attempted throughout this book to distinguish proprietary trademarks from descriptive terms by following the capitalization style used by the manufacturer.

SYBEX is not affiliated with any manufacturer.

Every effort has been made to supply complete and accurate information. However, SYBEX assumes no responsibility for its use, nor for any infringement of the intellectual property rights of third parties which would result from such use.

Library of Congress Card Number: 9386869

ISBN: 0-7821-1415-6

Manufactured in the United States of America

10 9 8 7 6 5 4 3 2 1

Dedicated to the memory of Rose Savage, from Russia with love.

▶ acknowledgments

While it is the author's job to put the words of a book on paper, producing a book is a task shared by many. An author could ask for no more support and professionalism than that provided by the fine staff of SYBEX.

Joanne Cuthbertson, coordinating editor, and Sarah Wadsworth, developmental editor, cultivated this book and ensured that it adhered to the excellent SYBEX tradition. Thanks also to Steve Lipson, whose contribution to the new ABCs format is greatly appreciated.

Armin Brott was responsible for editing the book. It was no easy task for Armin to convert a deluge of material to the final form you see here. His decisions were always on target.

Horace Shelton served as technical editor, with amazing speed and attention to detail. Val Potter coordinated our efforts, handling the flow of paperwork, disks, and problems between coasts.

My thanks to screen graphics specialists Cuong Le and Aldo Bermudez, typesetter Alissa Feinberg, production coordinator David Silva, indexer Nancy Guenther, and book designer Ingrid Owen, whose efforts translated the concept of this new format to reality. Thanks also Dr. Rudolph Langer, as well as the other people at SYBEX whose efforts contributed to this book.

Barbara Neibauer was responsible for keeping me awake, alert, and on track. She spent endless hours organizing papers, cheering me along, and providing the type of support that only a friend and wife could sustain.

▶ ▶ ▶ ▶ ▶ ▶ ▶

contents at a glance

table of contents

part two

EDITING YOUR WORK 37

▶ introduction

In the battle for the Windows word processing market, only the strong and daring will survive. With version 6.0 of Word for Windows, however, *we* are the real winners. To maintain its dominant market position, Microsoft has released this blockbuster program with more power, more features, more of everything we could ask for in a word processor.

Microsoft Word not only successfully combines a top-quality word processor and desktop publisher, it also is a first-class spreadsheet program, database manager, drawing program, and special effects font program.

Equipped with this book, you'll be using Word for Windows 6.0 to prepare documents of all types, and in ways you never thought possible. Don't worry about trudging through a lot of dense material or silly anecdotes—you'll be typing and printing documents in a few minutes.

Here's What You'll Get

To give the optimal benefits of Word, we've taken the best features of SYBEX's renowned ABCs books, fine-tuned them for Word's capabilities, and mixed our own blend of tips, tricks, and hints. Each key

Word function is covered in a short two-page lesson that gives you everything you'll need. Here's what you get in each lesson:

- ▶ A concise step-by-step guide that you can immediately apply to your own work—you don't have to type some silly document that's been made up for you. (But if you need some structured practice, you'll find it in this book as well!)

- ▶ A graphic showing what you'll see on the screen, or highlighting the capabilities of the function you are learning.

- ▶ Useful hints, tips, and tricks about the procedure. You'll learn how the function works as well as shortcuts and items to watch out for. Each item is marked with a small icon to help you decide which are important for you to read.

Before you dive in, be sure to look at the "Word for Windows Basics" section that follows this introduction. This short section shows you how to work with Word's menus and dialog boxes, and how to get around the Windows environment.

Once you are familiar with Word, you can use this book in several ways:

- ▶ Read this book from start to finish to learn Word 6.0 in a linear fashion. You'll begin with what you need to get started, and work your way to tables, newsletters, and even desktop publishing.

- ▶ Need a quick reference or refresher? Go directly to the step-by-step directions. At the beginning of each lesson is a handy reference showing where you'll read about key features.

- ▶ Something didn't go exactly as planned? Interested in more details? Check out the tips, tricks, or hints.

▶ Need a little hands-on practice to reinforce your skills? Do the optional exercises (*Let's Do It*) after each major part of the book.

Here's What You'll learn

We've divided this book into four parts to complement the way you work and learn. In Part One, you'll learn how to start Word and type, save, and print documents. You'll learn how to use and select Toolbars and how to change the way your documents are displayed. All this and more in two short lessons!

tip ▶ When you see this icon, you'll find a handy tip or short-cut for performing the task.

for more... ▶ When you want some more information, look for this icon. Here you'll find additional details about the task or a cross-reference to related lessons.

power bar ▶ This icon means you can perform the function quickly using a Toolbar.

oops! ▶ Refer to these notes to troubleshoot problems or to help you when something appears not to work properly.

new feature ▶ Special Word features are explained where you see this icon.

▶ ▶ ▶ ▶ ▶ ▶ ▶

With the basics under your belt, you'll learn how to edit documents in Part Two. There are lessons on opening documents, inserting and deleting text, correcting mistakes, and moving and copying text. You'll also learn how to enter text automatically, insert the date, repeat keystrokes, create templates for consistent documents, and use Word's Wizards to create professional-looking documents with a few clicks of the mouse. There's also a special section about using windows to work with several documents at a time.

Part Three concentrates on formatting. You'll learn how to change the appearance of text and how to insert symbols, icons, and foreign-language characters. There's a lesson on centering text, aligning it, changing line spacing, and setting tabs. You'll learn how to indent and hyphenate paragraphs, change margins and page sizes, and create envelopes automatically. Part Three also explains how to add headers, footers, and page numbers, how to format an entire document with a single click of the mouse, and how to surround paragraphs in boxes and highlight text with horizontal and vertical lines.

In Part Four you'll learn about some special Word features. After reading these lessons, you'll be able to create tables and newsletters, create form letters, and record macros. You'll learn how to work with styles to streamline formatting, how to check your spelling, even improve your vocabulary and grammar. Finally, you'll learn the basics of desktop publishing—how to add graphics, draw your own artwork, create charts and graphs, and create special effects with TrueType fonts.

At the end of each part, you'll find some short exercises (Let's Do It). These take you step-by-step through a sample document, performing the key tasks described in the book. Follow the exercises if you're not sure how something should work, or if you want to strengthen your skills before using them in your own documents.

▶ ▶ ▶ ▶ ▶ ▶ ▶

▶ Word Basics

With all of Word's power and versatility, it is still a re-markably easy—and even fun to use—program. If you have a mouse and are at all familiar with Microsoft Windows, you'll feel right at home with Word. As a Windows application, Word takes full advantage of the graphic interface and uses all of the user-friendly conventions for which Windows has become so popular.

If you are a new Word user, this section will show you how to communication with the program. You'll learn about the Word screen, how to give commands and how to select options using the mouse, keyboard, menus, and dialog boxes.

If you are an experienced Windows user, you'll immediately feel comfortable with Word. But read this section to learn about some new Word features.

If you have never used a Windows application before, or do not have a mouse, there is no need to feel intimidated by the following discussion of menus, mice, and dialog boxes. Just take your time working through this section until you feel comfortable with the Word screen. A little practice, and patience, will go a long way toward making you a confident Word user.

Using a Mouse with Word

Having a mouse is not an absolute necessity with Word, but it will make things easier to use. With a mouse, for example, you can just point to the function you want to perform and click the left mouse button. A mouse is particularly useful if you use graphics, since it allows you to change the size, shape, and position of graphics without a single keystroke!

There are several types of actions you can take with the mouse:

▶ To *point* means to place the mouse pointer on an object. While this is usually given in preparation for another mouse instruction, you can point to some Word objects to see its name or a brief description of its function.

▶ To *click* means to place the mouse pointer on an object, then quickly press and release the left mouse button.

▶ To *double-click* means to click twice. If you double-click and nothing happens, you did not click fast enough—try it again, but faster.

▶ To *drag* means to place the mouse pointer on an object, press and hold down the left mouse button, then move the mouse. Do not release the mouse button until you reach a specified location.

Using the Keyboard

Though it is certainly easier to use Word if you have a mouse, you can get by with the keyboard alone. Most commands and actions that can be performed with the mouse can also be performed with the keyboard.

In this book, keystrokes that should be pressed together are separated by a plus sign. The combination *Ctrl+X*, for example, means that you should press and *hold down* the Ctrl key, press and release the X key, then release the Ctrl key.

Other key combinations are pressed in sequence, one after the other. These are always separated by blank spaces. For example, *Alt+F P* means to press Alt+F, release both keys, then press and release the P key.

Conventions Used in this Book

Throughout this book you will get concise instructions on how to perform Word's functions. In most cases, you can follow the instructions whether or not you have a mouse.

Most instructions tell you to *select* an option. Selecting an item means to chose it in a way that performs some action. To select an item with the mouse, point to the item with the mouse pointer then *click* the left mouse button.

To *highlight* something means to place the cursor at the option so its name appears in reverse. Highlighting does not perform any action immediately but prepares the option for some action. Highlighting is usually performed with the keyboard to prepare an item for selection. For example, you can highlight a Menu Bar option without displaying its pull-down menu.

Often, you have to select more than one item to perform a Word function. Rather than tell you to *Select File, then select*

Print, then select Current Page, each of the items you must select are separated by the ➤ symbol, as in

Select File ➤ Print ➤ Current Page

This means to select these three items in turn as they appear on the screen.

Many Word options also have shortcut keys—key combinations you can press instead of selecting items from the screen. You'll see shortcut keys listed after the select instruction, like this:

Select File ➤ Open (Ctrl+O)

This means you can either select File then Open, or press Ctrl+O. The shortcut keys are most useful if you do not have a mouse. In addition, many of the shortcut keys are the same as those used for other Windows application. So, for example, if you know how to *cut and paste* text in one Windows program, you can use the same keystrokes to cut and paste text in Word.

While most lessons in this book show the keyboard shortcut keys, it is not practical to show all that are available. To help keyboard users, you'll find a list of shortcut keys on the inside covers of this book. The keystrokes are grouped according to the lesson where the function is discussed. Refer to the list while you are reading each lesson.

Understanding the Word for Windows Screen

When you start Word, the screen contains the *Title Bar, Menu Bar*, the *Standard Toolbar*, the *Formatting Toolbar*, and the *Ruler* at the top of the screen:

➤ The Title Bar will display the name of your document.

- ▶ The Menu Bar displays the menus from which you select the commands to work with your documents.

- ▶ The Standard Toolbar contains buttons for performing common word processing functions with a click of the mouse.

- ▶ The Formatting Toolbar contains buttons and list for formatting your document.

- ▶ The Ruler is used to set tabs, indent paragraphs, and change the page margins.

You can use the Menu Bar with either the mouse or the keyboard. You can only use the Toolbar buttons and Ruler if you have a mouse. If you do not have a mouse, you can use the pull-down menus in the Formatting Toolbar, but you must perform the Toolbar button functions using options in the Menu Bar.

At the bottom of the screen is the *Status Bar*. The Status Bar is divided into several sections. The first section, on the left, gives you information about the portion of text displayed on the screen:

Page—The number of the page you are currently viewing on the screen.

Sec—The section of the document you are viewing. You can divide a document into sections to use multiple page formats in one document.

1/1—The current page and the total number of pages in the document. The notation 2/5, for examples, means you are on the second page of a five page document.

The next section tells you where on the page the insertion point (the cursor) is located:

At—The distance the current line is from the top of the page.

Ln—The line number where the insertion point is located.

Col—The character position from the left margin.

Next, you'll see the current time. Word displays the time so you can keep track of your progress.

Following the time, you'll see the mode display. The dimmed characters means that the modes are currently turned off. When you activate a mode, its characters will become darker indicating that the mode is turned on:

REC—The record macro function is on.

MRK—Revision markings in on.

EXT—Text selection is on.

OVR—Overtype mode is on.

WPH—Word Help mode is on.

Error:
Word~~Perfect~~
Help mode
is on

The area between the Ruler and Status Bar is the text window. The text window is where your document appears as you type. The small horizontal line in the window is called the *endmark*. The endmark indicates the end of your document, and moves down as you insert text, up as you delete text. The blinking vertical line is called the *insertion point*. The insertion point is the Windows equivalent to a cursor, since it indicates the position of the next characters typed or deleted. You can use either

the mouse or the directional arrow keys to move the insertion point to the place where you want to type, insert, or delete characters. You can position the insertion point to the left or right of a character, but not directly on it.

If you have a mouse, you will also see a *mouse pointer*. The shape of the pointer depends where it is on the screen. When it is in the typing window, the pointer is usually shaped like an I-beam. The pointer will change to an arrow when you point to the Menu Bar or a Toolbar, or to other shapes depending on the action you are going to perform.

Working with Menus

Selecting a Menu Bar option with the mouse or keyboard displays a *pull-down menu*. A pull-down menu lists specific operations that you can perform. Figure B.1, for instance, shows the pull-down menu for the File option. Notice that the first option on the menu is *highlighted*, or appears in reverse. This means that it is ready to select or activate. In some pull-down menus, certain options may appear gray, or *dimmed*. These options are not currently available to be selected but must first be activated by performing some other function.

If the function has an alternate shortcut key, it will be listed next to the command, such as Ctrl+S next to the menu option Save.

An ellipses (…) next to the command means that selecting the option will display a dialog box containing additional choices from which you must select. A checkmark indicates that the option is turned on or selected.

Here's how to use menus:

- ▶ To display a pull-down menu, click on the option with the left mouse button, or hold down the Alt key and press the underlined letter of the function.

Menu Bar with
pull-down
menu for the
File option

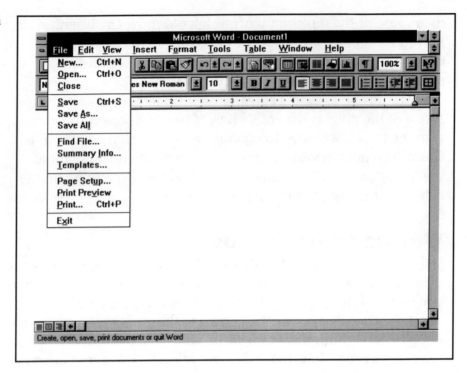

fig B·1·

- ▶ To display another pull-down menu, click on another
  Menu Bar option, or press the → or ← keys.

- ▶ To select a pull-down menu option, click on the option with
  the mouse button, press the underlined letter, or press the ↓
  or ↑ key to highlight the option and press Enter.

- ▶ To cancel a menu, click elsewhere on the window or press
  the Esc key.

Working with Dialog Boxes

Selecting a menu item or performing a function may display
a dialog box. A *dialog box* contains additional options and

requires some type of input by either clicking the mouse or typing on the keyboard. While some dialog boxes only present a few options, others can be quite complex.

All dialog boxes have a Title Bar that gives the name of the box, indicating the overall function its options perform. Many dialog boxes in Word appear like a series of index cards, as shown in Figure B.2. Each card has a tab on top that names the category of options it contains. Clicking on the tab brings the options on the card into the foreground. With the keyboard, select a tab by pressing Alt and the underlined letter on the tab. The dialog box shown in Figure B.2, for example, shows two tabs: Labels and Envelopes.

The box itself contains a number of different types of options.

B.2 is overleaf though I can't see where it's labelled B.2

Moving within a Dialog Box

Move from item to item in a dialog box by clicking the mouse in the item you want to change.

With the keyboard, press Tab to move forward, Shift+Tab to move backward through the options. You can also press Alt and the underlined letter of the option you want to select.

Check Boxes

A *check box* is a small square next to an option that you may select. When you select a check box, Word places an X in the box indicating that the option is turned on. Selecting a check box that already contains an X, will turn off the option, removing the X. Click on a check box or the option name next to the box to insert or delete the X. With the keyboard, press Alt and the underlined letter of the command.

For example, Figure B.2 shows two check boxes—Use Return Address and Delivery Point Bar Code. To select Use Return

Envelopes and
Labels dialog
box

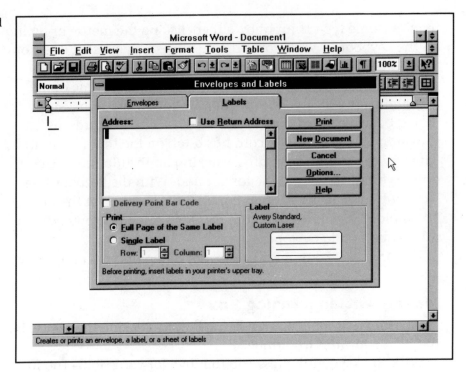

fig B.2

Address, click on the checkbox or anywhere on the words Use
Return Address. With the keyboard, press Alt+R.

Note that the Delivery Point Bar Code options is dimmed and
contains no underlined selection character. This is because an
address must be entered first to make the options selectable.

In many cases, check boxes are grouped together. Within the
group, they are usually non-exclusive so you can check more
than one box at a time. In a few cases, checkboxes will be exclusive within a group—turning one on will turn another off.

When you format characters, for example, you can select either the subscript or superscript checkbox but not both.

With the keyboard, select a checkbox by pressing Alt and the underlined letter of the option.

Option Buttons

An *option button* is a circle that represents an exclusive setting—only one button in a group can be selected at a time. Selecting one button automatically turns off any other selected. Figure B.2 shows a group of two option buttons in the Print section of the dialog box—Full Page of the Same Label and Single Label. You can only select one option in the group.

Select an option button the same as a check box. When the button is turned on, the center circle will be filled in.

Text Boxes

A *text box* is an area where you can type information using the keyboard. Move into a text box by clicking it with the mouse, by pressing Alt and the underlined letter, or using the Tab or Shift+Tab keys. Then, type the value or setting you want for that option.

In Figure B.2, the Address box is a large text box for entering the address to be placed on a label. To type an address, you click anywhere in the box or press Alt+A.

The dialog box also contains two smaller text boxes, Row and Column. These box are dimmed until you select the Single Label feature. Note that the Row and Column boxes have up and down-pointing arrows on the right. These indicate that you can increase or decrease the value in the box by clicking on the arrows.

Drop-Down List Boxes

An option that has a small down-pointing arrow above a horizontal line contains a drop-down list box. A *drop-down list box* stores options that you can quickly select to insert in the box. Figure B.3 shows two options with drop down list boxes. Notice that each contains the option name, such as Tray and Label Products, and a box that contains the current setting.

To display the list box, click on the arrow. With the keyboard, press the number next to the item, or move to the item and press Enter. When the list appears, select an item by clicking on it with the mouse or by highlighting it with the arrow keys. Remove the list box by double-clicking on the selected item, clicking elsewhere in the dialog box, or moving to another dialog box option.

If a list box is not large enough to display all of the options, it will have a Scroll Bar on the right. You use the Scroll Bars to display additional choices. In Lesson 3 you'll learn how to use Scroll Bars.

In some cases, there will be a space between the down arrow and the box that contains the current setting. This is a combination text box and drop down list box. You can either type your setting into the text box, or select an item from the list. When there is no space between the between the box and the arrow, as in Figure B.3, you can only select an item from the list, you cannot type directly in the box.

Figure B.3 also shows a list that is already displayed on the screen, Product Number. Select an option in the box by clicking on it with the mouse or highlight it using the arrow keys.

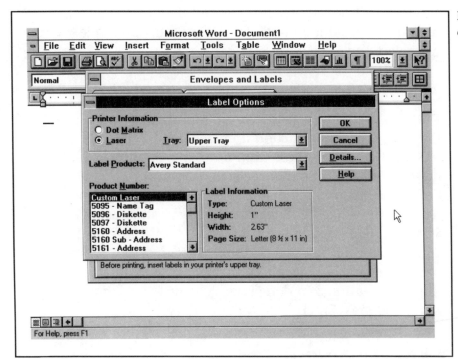

Labels Options dialog box

fig. B.3.

Previews and Information Panels

Many dialog boxes affect the appearance or format of text. Most of these dialog boxes will contain a preview panel showing the effects of your selections on the document. In Figure B.2, for example, the drawing of a label in the Label panel will depend on your settings in the Options dialog box.

The dialog box in Figure B.3 contains an information label, called Label Information. The information in the panel will change as you select options.

Before exiting a dialog box, look at the preview panel, or read the information panel, to confirm that you made the correct selections.

Commands

Dialog boxes will also contain commands. Selecting a command performs some action immediately.

Most dialog boxes have commands in rectangular buttons labeled *OK*, *Cancel*, and *Help*. Selecting OK accepts the settings in the dialog box and removes it from the screen. Selecting Cancel removes the dialog box but ignores any changes you've made. Selecting Help displays information about the options in the dialog box. With the keyboard, press Esc to accept cancel, or press F1 to get help information. To accept OK, move to the command button so a dotted box surrounds the command word, and press Enter.

Shortcut Menus

Word has added frequently used menu options to Shortcut menus. A Shortcut menu appears when you press the right mouse pointer. The options displayed in the menu depends where you are pointing to when you press the mouse button.

By using a Shortcut menu, you can perform common functions without having to move the mouse all of the way to the top of the screen to reach the Menu Bar.

You learn about Shortcut menus in the lessons that follow. However, as you work with Word, experiment on your own by pointing to an object or area of the screen and pressing the right mouse button.

With the keyboard, you can display a Shortcut menu by pressing Shift+F10. Close the menu by pressing Esc.

1 part one

QUICK START

Word for Windows is a wonder. Powerful and versatile, Word can be used everywhere: in the home and in school, in a small business or the largest international conglomerate.

But Word is also easy and fun to use. To prove this point, in the two short lessons that follow, you will learn how to type, save, and print documents, and how to use Word's fascinating interface.

It's So Easy

Starting Word for Windows

The tasks in this lesson will get you started with Word for Windows by teaching you the most basic features. You'll learn how to start Word, how to enter text, how to get on-screen help, how to change the display mode and magnification, and more.

If you have not yet installed Word on your computer, carefully follow the installation instructions supplied with the program, then come back to this lesson. If Word for Windows is already on your computer, you're ready to go!

▼   ▼   ▼   ▼   ▼

STARTING WORD FOR WINDOWS

Starting Word for Windows is easy. Just make sure that you or someone else has installed Word and Windows on your computer's hard disk drive, and that your computer, monitor, and printer are all set up as they should be.

To start Word:

1 Turn on your computer and monitor.

2 If Windows doesn't start automatically, type WIN and press Enter to run it.

The Word for Windows screen

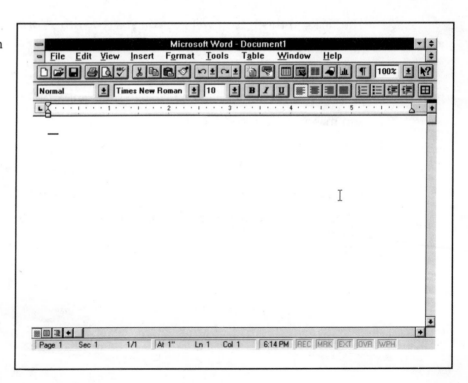

3 Double-click on the Microsoft Word icon in the Microsoft Applications group window.

4 A dialog box will appear with a handy Tip of the Day. The tip will change each time you start Word. Read the tip, then select OK.

The Tip of the Day reminds you of many of the shortcuts Word offers. However, if you do not want a tip to appear when you start Word, click on the Show Tips on Startup box in the Tip window.

oops! ▷ **Something's Wrong**
If the Microsoft Applications group window is not displayed when Windows starts, select **Window** from the Menu Bar, then click on **Microsoft Applications** in the pull-down list.

tip ▷ **If you're ready to quit**
If you are not ready to continue with this lesson, select File ➤ Exit (or press Alt+F4). If you entered any text on the screen, a dialog box will appear asking if you want to save the document. Select No.

▲ ▲ ▲ ▲ ▲ ▲

TYPING IN
WORD FOR WINDOWS

If you've ever used a typewriter, you'll feel at home in Word. All of the letter, number, and punctuation keys on the four middle rows of the keyboard work just the same.

To type a document:

1 Press Tab to insert a tab at the start of a paragraph.

2 Type until you reach the end of the paragraph. Do not press Enter when you reach the end of a line. Word senses when the word you are typing will not fit in the line and

Word moved the word automatically to the next line as it was typed

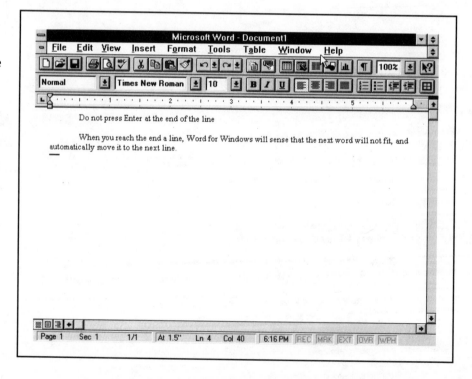

moves the word to the next line automatically, as shown in the figure. This process is called "word-wrap."

3 Press Enter to end a paragraph or to insert a blank line.

4 Press Backspace to erase mistakes.

As you type, the insertion point (cursor) moves down the page and the Ln indicator in the status line changes. As you pass the last line on the screen the lines at the top scroll up out of view. You can use the Scroll Bars to bring text back into view, as explained in the Lesson 3.

tip ▶ **Is there still room on the page?**
When you reach the end of a page just continue typing—Word automatically starts new pages as necessary. A dotted line appears across the screen, and the Page indicator in the Status Bar increases by one.

for more... ▶ **Taking control of pages**
If you want to end one page and begin another before Word changes pages automatically, press Ctrl+Enter. See "Inserting Page Breaks" in Lesson 6 for more information.

▲ ▲ ▲ ▲ ▲ ▲

GETTING HELP

With a program as powerful as Word, it is easy to forget how some features work. To help jog your memory, Word has an on-screen Help system. Word Help includes information on menu commands, dialog boxes, and other tools. There are even demonstrations that take you step-by-step through complete word processing tasks.

Getting help from Word:

| Select Help to display the Help pull down menu.

Help Contents
window

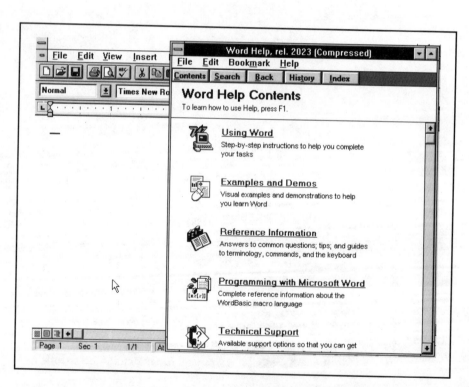

2　To see detailed information, do *one* of the following:

▶　Select Contents to display a list of general topics for which help is available, then double-click on the subject you want help with—scroll the list if necessary.

▶　Select Search for Help On to select from a list of help topics, or to enter the subject for which you need help.

▶　Select Examples and Demos to display a list of topics for which Word provides step-by-step illustrations.

3　Double-click on the Help window control box (or press Alt+F4) to quit the Help system.

---

tip ▷　**Skip the menu, full speed ahead**

For context-sensitive help, click on the Help button in the standard Toolbar, then click on the Toolbar button or menu item you want help on. With the keyboard, highlight the item, then press F1. Word will display a screenful of help information on the highlighted item.

arning! ▷　**One-touch Help**

Click on the Help button in the Toolbar to access the Help menu.

▲ ▲ ▲ ▲ ▲ ▲

SELECTING AND DISPLAYING TOOLBARS

Some functions are performed so often when creating documents, that Word has added them to special Toolbars. The Toolbars allow you to complete a function with a single click of the mouse. By default, you will see the Standard Toolbar, the Formatting Toolbar, and the Ruler. When you place the mouse pointer on any Toolbar button, Word displays the name of the button in a small box under the pointer, and a description of the button is displayed in the Status Bar. When you perform some functions, such as outlining, Word will automatically display a specialized Toolbar for that task.

To use a Toolbar:

▶ Click on the button of the desired function.

To hide and display Toolbars:

1 Point to a Toolbar and click the right mouse button to display the Shortcut menu shown in the figure.

2 Select the Toolbar you want to hide or display.

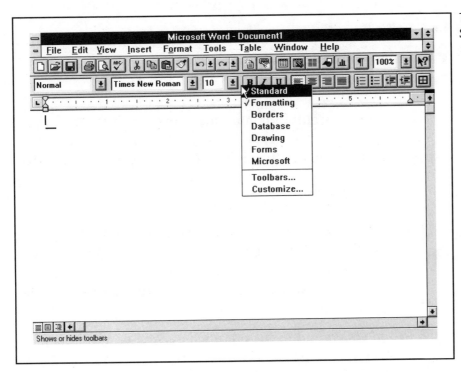

Toolbar
Shortcut menu

tip ▶ **It remembers!**

The Toolbars that appear on screen when you exit Word will automatically appear when you next start Word. If you do not want a Toolbar to appear, remove it before exiting Word.

for more... ▶ **To learn more about the Ruler**

You use the Ruler to adjust the margins, paragraph indentations, and to set tabs. You'll learn more the ruler in Lesson 9.

▲ ▲ ▲ ▲ ▲ ▲

CHANGING THE APPEARANCE OF TOOLBARS

Toolbars are so useful that you may want to adjust their appearance to better suit the way you work. You can move a Toolbar to another position on the screen, and you can change the size and appearance of the buttons.

To move a Toolbar:

1 Point to a blank area in the Toolbar, then start dragging the Toolbar to its new location. (Remember, to drag, click the left mouse button *and hold it down* while moving the mouse.) As you drag, a dotted representation of the Toolbar will move along with it.

2 When you've put the Toolbar where you want it to be, release the mouse button.

To change the appearance of the Toolbar:

1 Select Toolbars from the Toolbar shortcut menu, or select View ➤ Toolbars.

2 Select Color Buttons to toggle between color and black and white buttons; select Large Buttons to increase the size of the buttons; select Show Tooltip to toggle on or off the display of the button name under the mouse.

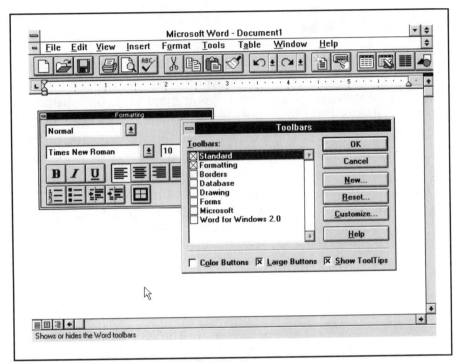

Toolbars
dialog box with customized Toolbar in the background

for more... ▶ **Using buttons**

See later lessons to learn about the functions performed by these Button Bars.

tip ▶ **Toolbar shapes**

If you drag the mouse to the top, bottom or either side of the screen, the Toolbar will appear in one row or column. Drag the mouse within the window to create a rectangular Toolbar. You can change the size of the rectangular Toolbar by dragging one of its borders.

13

▼ ▼ ▼ ▼ ▼

CHANGING VIEWS

Word has four view modes: Normal, Outline, Page Layout, and Master Document. When you first start Word, it will be in Normal view. In Normal view, you'll see fonts and graphics (although graphics will not appear in their exact position in relation to text), but you won't see headers, footers, page numbers, and margin areas. In Page Layout view, you'll see the document exactly how it will appear when printed, and a ruler will appear down the left side of the screen.

You can type, edit, and format documents in all four views. To change to Normal view:

► Select View ➤ Normal.

Document in Page Layout view showing a header, fonts and graphics

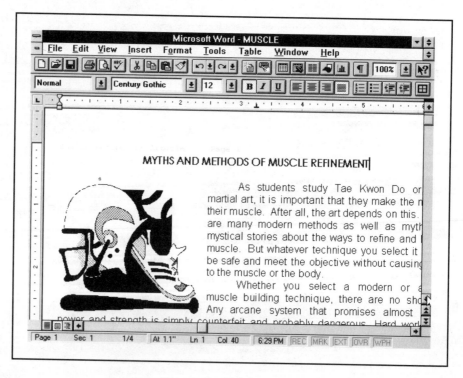

To change to Page Layout view:

▶ Select View ➤ Page Layout.

To change to Outline view:

▶ Select View ➤ Outline.

To change to Master Document view:

▶ Select View ➤ Master Document.

The figure on the facing page shows a document in Page Layout view.

tip ▷ **Full-screen display**
If you find the Toolbars and other screen elements distracting, you can remove them all in one step by selecting View ➤ Full Screen. A small icon labeled Full will appear in the bottom right corner—click on the icon to return the screen to its normal display.

tip ▷ **Using views**
Use Outline view to create outlines and organize documents. Use Master Document view when working with large documents that are divided into sections.

new feature ▷ **Click views**
Use the three buttons on the left of the horizontal Scroll Bar to change views. They are (from the left) Normal, Page Layout, and Outline views.

▲ ▲ ▲ ▲ ▲ ▲ ▲

CHANGING THE DISPLAY MAGNIFICATION

The default display magnification is set at 100%. This means that the text and graphics appear about the same size on screen as they do on the printed page. You can change the magnification to display a full page or more on screen at one time, or to enlarge the text to make it easier to read. For example, when set at 200%, the display is twice the printed size.

You can edit and format your document no matter what magnification you select.

Zoom Control list with two pages displayed

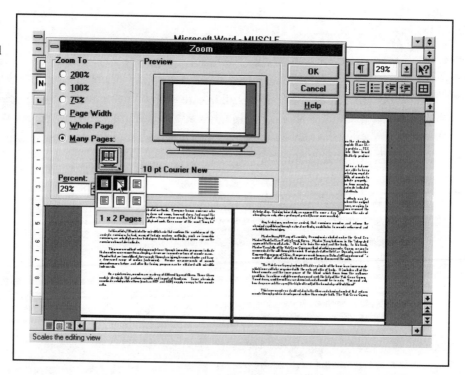

To change the magnification:

1 Select View ➤ Zoom to display the Zoom dialog box.

2 Select a percentage. The options are 200%, 100%, 75%, Page Width, Whole Page, and Many Pages. You can also set a custom magnification between 10% and 200%. Whole Page and Many pages are dimmed in Normal view.

3 Select OK.

In Page Layout view, select Many Pages to display a thumbnail display of two or more pages on the screen. Click on the icon of the monitor to determine the number of pages displayed.

arning! ▶ **Instant zoom**

You can also zoom by pulling down the Zoom Control button in the Standard Toolbar. The options are 200%, 175%, 100%, 75%, 50%, 25%, 10%, and Page Width. In Page Layout view, the list also includes **Whole Page** and **Two Pages**.

tip ▶ **Zoom options**

Page Width adjusts the magnification so you can see the full line of text on the screen. Full Page displays a entire page on screen.

▲ ▲ ▲ ▲ ▲ ▲

It's So Easy

▶ Printing and Saving Documents

When you are done typing a document, you'll need to print it or save it to a disk so you can use it later. Usually, you'll do both. Even in this age of electronic mail, printed copies are handy for reviewing documents and for distributing your documents to others. You will still need to save a document if you want to edit or print it later.

▶ ▶ ▶ ▶ ▶ ▶ ▶ ▶ ▶

▼ ▼ ▼ ▼ ▼

SAVING A DOCUMENT

When you save a document for the first time, you must give it a name. Document names can be from one to eight characters long, plus a three-character extension.

To save your document for the first time:

1 Select File ➤ Save As or File ➤ Save (Ctrl+S) to display the Save As dialog box.

2 Type a document name. When Word saves a document, it automatically adds the extension DOC. If you want

Save As dialog box

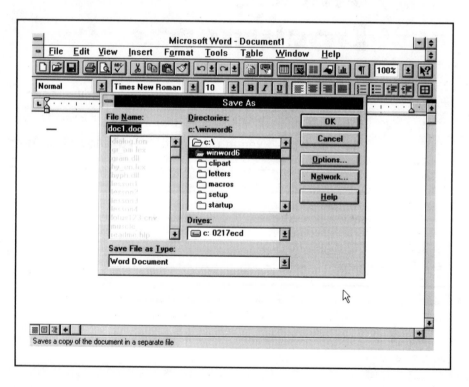

another extension, or want to save the file on another disk or directory, type a full path and filename, as in

c:\BUDGET\REPORT.TXT

3 Select OK. The document's name will appear in the Title Bar.

Once you have saved your document, you can save it again by selecting File ➤ Save (Ctrl+S). The Save As dialog box will not appear.

warning! ▷ **Quick document saving**

Click on the Save button to save a document.

tip ▷ **If you use another version of Word**

Word saves documents in a format incompatible with earlier versions of Word. If you want to use the document with Word for DOS, or another word processing program, select File ➤ Save As, pull down the Save Files as Type list box, and select the desired format.

oops! ▷ **Don't be lazy**

Word saves a temporary copy of your document every 10 minutes. This is only a safeguard in the event of a power or computer failure. *You must still save your document yourself before exiting Word.*

▲ ▲ ▲ ▲ ▲ ▲

▼　▼　▼　▼　▼

CLEARING THE
DOCUMENT WINDOW

Saving a document does not clear it from the screen. This allows
you to save your text and continue working on it.

If you have already saved one document and want to work
on another, or you have changed your mind about what you've
already typed and want to start all over again, you can clear
the screen using the File ➤ Close command.

To clear the typing window:

| Select File ➤ Close.

Word screen
after closing
open documents

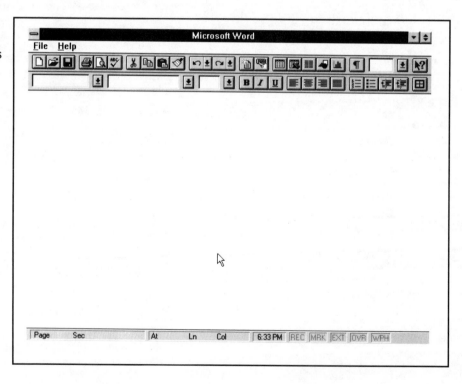

2 If you made any changes to the document since you last saved it, a dialog box will appear asking if you want to save the document before exiting. Select Yes to save the document, No not to save it, or Cancel to leave the document on screen.

3 The Menu Bar will display just the File and Help options, and the ruler and scroll bars will disappear, as shown in the figure. You cannot type a document in this mode.

4 Click on the New button in the Toolbar to open a blank document window.

tip ▶ Using the File menu

When you close the document, you can start a new document by selecting File ➤ New, then clicking on OK in the dialog box that appears.

tip ▶ Using the control box

You can also close a document by double-clicking on its control box. The document control box (which looks like a small rectangle) is on the left side of the Menu Bar, beneath the Word control box (a larger rectangle) in the Title Bar. Double-clicking on the Word control box will close Word.

▲ ▲ ▲ ▲ ▲ ▲

▶ ▶ ▶

▼　▼　▼　▼　▼

PREVIEWING A DOCUMENT BEFORE PRINTING

In addition to the four view modes, you can display your document in Print Preview. Print Preview displays one or more entire pages at one time. You can adjust the left and right margins, and move text up or down on the page. Use print preview to make minor changes to the overall page layout.

To Print Preview:

❙ Select File ➤ Print Preview. The figure shows a document in Print Preview display.

Document in
Preview mode

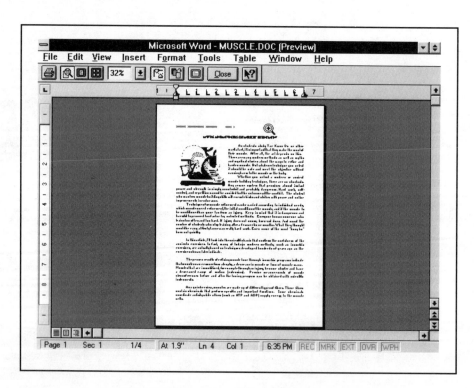

2 The mouse pointer will appear as a small magnifying lens. To quickly enlarge a portion of the page, click on the text you want to enlarge.

3 Select Close to return to the previous view.

While you can use the vertical and horizontal Rulers to change the margins and layout of the page, the small display makes it difficult to judge the effects of the changes.

new feature ▶ **Toolbar options**

The Print Preview Toolbar has these options: *Print*: prints the document. *Magnifier*: changes from magnification mode to editing mode. *One Page*: displays one page. *Multiple Pages*: displays several pages. *Zoom*: changes the displayed magnification. *View Ruler*: toggles on and off the ruler display. *Shrink to fit*: makes Word attempt to adjust the spacing to reduce the number of pages. *Full screen*: displays the document full screen. *Close*: exits Print Preview. *Help*: displays help information.

▲ ▲ ▲ ▲ ▲ ▲

▶ ▶ ▶

▼ ▼ ▼ ▼ ▼

PRINTING DOCUMENTS

Word has many powerful printing features. You can print just the page you are working on, a bit of selected text, a series of selected pages, or the whole document. You can print just the odd or even pages, or print the document to a file on disk. You can print multiple copies, and you select to print them collated. When collated, each copy of a multiple page document is printed separately, rather than multiple copies of individual pages.

Print dialog box

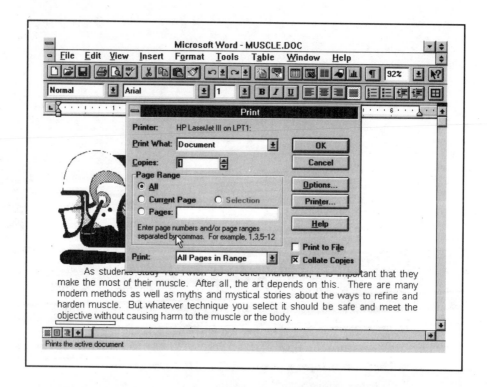

But if you just want a quick copy of your document, the process is easy. To print a document:

1 Make sure your printer is turned on and ready, and that you have paper.

2 Select File ➤ Print (or press Ctrl+P) to display the Print dialog box.

3 Select OK.

One click printing

Click the **Print** button to print a document immediately without displaying the Print dialog box.

tip

Just to be safe, save!

You do not have to save a document before you print it. However, get into the habit of saving documents whether you print them or not. You may print a document, then need it again at some later time.

SELECTING YOUR PRINTER

If your document does not print accurately, you may have the wrong printer selected for printing with Word. Word for Windows can use any printer that has been set up for the Windows environment, even print drivers for fax transmission.

To select a printer:

1 Select File ➤ Print.

2 Click on the Printer button. A dialog box appears listing your installed Windows printers.

3 Double-click on the printer you want to use.

4 Select Close.

To use the printer for all documents, click on Set as Default Printer.

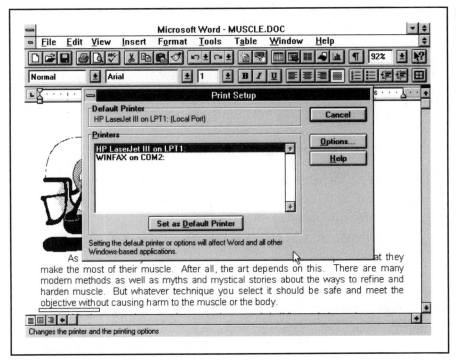

Select Printer
dialog box

oops! ► Your printer isn't listed

If your printer is not listed in the Select Printer dialog
box, you must install a printer using the Windows Control
Panel. If you cannot find your model printer, try selecting
a compatible brand. For dot matrix printers, try an **EPSON**
or **IBM Graphics** printer. For a laser printer, try one of
the **HP Laserjet** models. If you cannot find a substitute,
contact Microsoft Corporation for updated drivers and
printer information.

▼   ▼   ▼   ▼   ▼

QUITTING WORD

When you are finished using Word, exit the program and return to the Windows Program Manager. You can save a document and exit Word using a single dialog box.

To exit Word:

1 Select File ➤ Exit (Alt+F4).

2 If you made any changes to the document since you last saved it, a dialog box will appear asking if you want to save the document before closing. Select Yes to save the document, No not to save it, or Cancel to remain in Word.

File menu

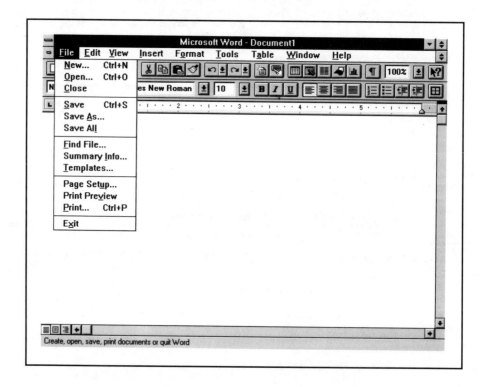

tip ▶ **Play it safe**
Always exit Word and Windows before turning off your computer. If you don't, you could damage files that you'll need later.

tip ▶ **Using the control box**
You can also exit Word by double-clicking on the Word window control box.

Typing documents in Word for Windows is really easy. Here is a brief exercise that lets you try out creating, saving, and printing a document.

1 Start Word for Windows.

2 Press Tab to indent the first paragraph.

3 Type the following text. Remember, do not press Enter when you reach the end of the line.

> **Vital signs are a series of measurements which indicate a person's general medical condition. The four principal measurements are blood pressure, pulse, respiration, and temperature. Because these measurements are often used as the first step in clinical diagnosis, they must be taken accurately, recorded, and reported promptly.**

4 Press Enter twice—once to end the paragraph, a second time to insert a blank line between paragraphs.

5 Press Tab, then type the next paragraph.

In some cases, the apical pulse is also considered a principal vital sign. This pulse is measured with a stethoscope so that the heart beat can be counted. The apical pulse is frequently measured on persons who have very rapid pulse rates, such as infants and young children.

Now let's save the document under the name *Vital.*

6 Select File ➤ Save As, or press Ctrl+S.

7 Type **VITAL**.

8 Select OK. Figure 1.1 shows the complete document.

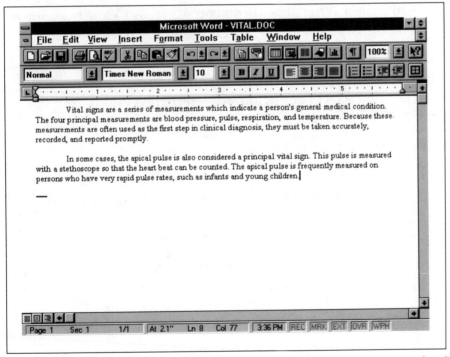

Figure 1.1:
VITAL.DOC

Now, print the document.

9 Select File ➤ Print, then select OK.

Let's use the View menu and the Zoom command to look at the document in several ways.

10 Select View ➤ Page Layout. Remember, you can also use the view buttons on the left of the status line—clicking on the center button changes to page Layout view. Notice the ruler now along the left side of the screen.

11 Pull down the Zoom Control button in the standard Toolbar and select Whole Page. You can also select View ➤ Zoom ➤ Whole Page ➤ OK. The text is too small to read, so let's change the zoom to see the full text.

12 Pull down the Zoom Control button on the standard Toolbar and select Page Width (or select Page Width from the Zoom dialog box).

13 Select File ➤ Print Preview.

14 Study the screen, then select the Close button in the Print Preview Toolbar, or select File ➤ Print Preview again.

15 Select View ➤ Normal.

Now let's change to full screen mode to see how Word looks without any menus or Toolbars.

16 Select View ➤ Full Screen.

17 Press Esc or click on the Full icon.

Since we are done with the document for now, close the screen and display a new blank window.

18 Select File ➤ Close.

19 Select File ➤ New ➤ OK, or click on the New button in the standard Toolbar.

20 Select File ➤ Exit.

That's all there is to it!

part two

EDITING YOUR WORK

So what if you make a few mistakes? With Word, you can edit your document, making it perfect, *before* you print it. In fact, Word will even correct some of your mistakes as you're making them!

In the lessons that follow, you'll learn all about editing your documents. You'll learn how to delete unwanted text, insert new text, and how to get the most from Word's editing capabilities.

It's So Easy

Recalling and Editing Documents

One of the best things about word processing is that you can edit a document as much as you want before printing it. You can print as many draft copies as you want and fine-tune the document—then print the final copy. In this lesson, you'll learn how to open documents you've saved and use some of Word's basic editing techniques.

OPENING A RECENTLY USED DOCUMENT

You can edit new documents as you type them or existing documents you've already saved. To edit an existing document, you must first *open* it, or recall it from the disk. Word makes it easy to open the last four documents you opened or created and saved.

To open a recently used document:

❙ Select File. At the bottom of the File menu, Word lists the last four documents you worked on. If the document is not

File menu
listing recently
used documents

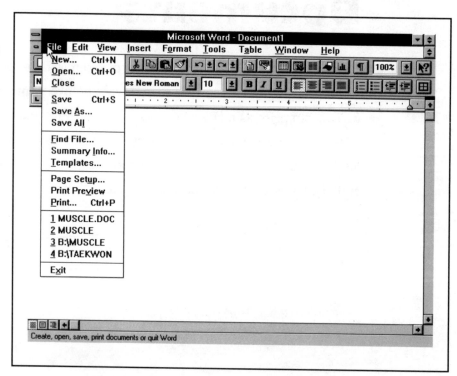

in the current directory, the complete path will be shown with the file name.

2 Click on the name of the file you want to open, or press the number next to the filename.

oops! ▶ **Cannot open the file**

If you deleted the file from your disk, Word will display an error message when you try to open it. Click on OK, or press Enter, to remove the error message from the screen.

for more... ▶ **What happened?**

If you already have a document in the window and open another, Word will open a new window for the second document. The first document window will be moved to the background. See "Opening Multiple Documents" in Lesson 7.

▼ ▼ ▼ ▼ ▼

OPENING A DOCUMENT

To open a document not listed in the File menu, use the File Open command. With File Open, you can open a document no matter where it is located on your disk or when you last worked on it.

To open a document:

1 Select File ➤ Open (Ctrl+O). Word displays the Open dialog box as shown in the figure. Word lists files with the .DOC extension.

2 Double-click on the file you want to open, or highlight the name of the file, then click on OK.

Open dialog box

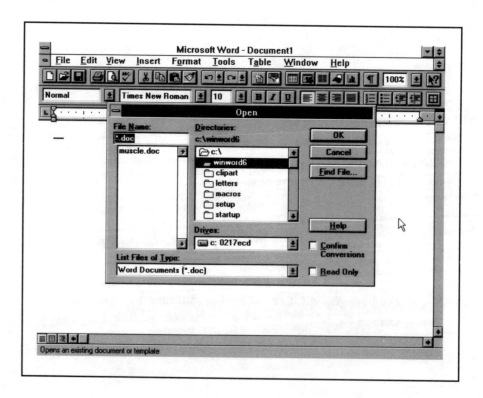

3 If the file you want to open is not listed, do one of the following:

▶ Type the complete path and name of the file in the File Name text box, then select OK.

▶ Select another directory in the Directories list box—double-click on the root directory (C:\) to list the directories on the drive.

▶ Select All Files (*.*) in the List Files of Type list.

Warning! ▶ **One click opening**

Click on the Open button to display the Open dialog box.

new feature ▶ **File conversions**

If you open a document that was created with another word processor, Word will automatically convert it to Word. When you save the file, you can save it in Word, or in the document's original format.

tip ▶ **Open options**

Select *Read Only* to prevent changing a document you just want to read or print. If you edit the document, the Save As dialog box will appear and you will have to enter a new name.

▲ ▲ ▲ ▲ ▲ ▲

INSERTING TEXT

To insert characters in text you've already typed, you must move the insertion point to the area of the document you want to change. When you enter characters within existing text, words to the right will move over and down to make room.

To move the insertion point:

▶ Place the mouse pointer where you want to enter, delete, or revise text, and then click the left button.

Insertion Point Movement Keys

KEY COMBINATION	PLACEMENT
→, ←, ↓, ↑	In the direction of the arrow
Ctrl+→	To the beginning of the next word
Ctrl+←	To the beginning of the current word, then to the previous word
Home	Beginning of the line
End	End of the line
Ctrl+PgUp	Top of the screen
Ctrl+PgDn	Bottom of the screen

tip ▶ **I thought you said it would insert**
By default, Word is in the *Insert* mode. If you press the Ins
key, new characters typed will replace existing ones. You
can also double-click on the OVR indicator to toggle insert
on and off.

oops! ▶ **All I get is numbers**
If you press an arrow key and a number appears on the
screen, press the key marked **Num Lock**. This turns off the
numeric function.

▲ ▲ ▲ ▲ ▲ ▲

USING THE SCROLL BARS

To move the insertion point to a part of the document that is not displayed, you must use the Scroll Bars.

▶ To scroll line by line, click the up or down arrow on the ends of the Scroll Bar.

▶ To scroll screen by screen, click above or below the scroll box—the box within the bar, between the up and down arrows.

▶ To scroll to a relative position in the document, drag the scroll box. For example, drag the box to the middle of the Scroll Bar to display text from the middle of the document.

▶ In Page Layout view, to scroll page by page, click on the previous or next page buttons (the double triangles) at the bottom of the Scroll Bar.

Use the Scroll Bar at the bottom of the window to scroll left and right.

Scrolling Keys

KEY COMBINATION	PLACEMENT
Ctrl+Home	Beginning of the document
Ctrl+End	End of the document
PgUp	Up one screen
PgDn	Down one screen
Alt+Ctrl+PgUp	Top of the previous page
Alt+Ctrl+PgDn	Top of the next page

oops! ▶

Where's the cursor?

Scrolling the screen with the Scroll Bar does not move the insertion point. The Page indicator in the Status Bar will show the number of the page being displayed but the At, Ln, and Col indicators will be blank. After scrolling the screen, click where you want to insert or edit text. If you do not click the mouse, the screen will scroll back to its previous location when you begin typing.

tip ▶

Using Goto

To quickly move to a specific page, select Edit ➤ Goto. A dialog box appears in which you can select to go a specific page or line on the page.

▲ ▲ ▲ ▲ ▲ ▲

It's So Easy

Editing Techniques

The ability to edit a document is what gives word processing its power and versatility. You can type a document,
letting your thoughts flow onto the screen, without
having to worry about making mistakes or arranging your
ideas on the page. Then, when you've gotten everything
down on paper, you can go back over the document
and edit it into the final form.

SELECTING TEXT

For many editing functions, you must select text, or *highlight* it, which makes the characters appear light on a dark background. Once you select text, you can easily delete it, copy it, move it to another location, or change its appearance.

To select text by dragging the mouse:

1 Place the mouse pointer at one end of the text.

2 Hold down the left mouse button.

3 Move the pointer while you hold down the left button.

4 Release the mouse button.

Selected text

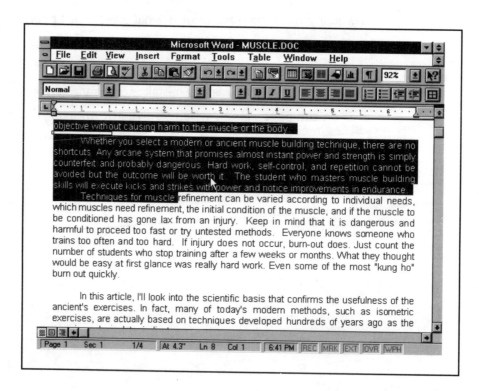

To select text by clicking the mouse:

▶ Point to a word and click twice to select it; click three times to select the entire paragraph.

▶ Click in the left margin once to select the line, twice to select the paragraph, three times to select the document, or drag the mouse to select consecutive lines.

To deselect all highlighted text quickly, just click the mouse.

tip ▶ **Selecting with the keyboard**
You can also select text by holding down the Shift key and moving the arrow keys.

oops! ▶ **Where did it go?**
If you press any character key when text is selected, the text will be deleted. If this is not what you intended, use the Undo command as explained later in this Lesson.

tip ▶ **Printing selected portions of your document**
Select the text you want to print, select File ➤ Print, click on Selection in the Print Range section, then click on OK.

▼ ▼ ▼ ▼ ▼

DELETING TEXT

Word provides many ways to delete characters or erase mistakes.

To delete text:

▶ To erase characters to the left of the insertion point, press the Backspace key.

▶ To erase a character to the right of the insertion point, press the Del key.

Shortcut menu displayed when pointing to selected text

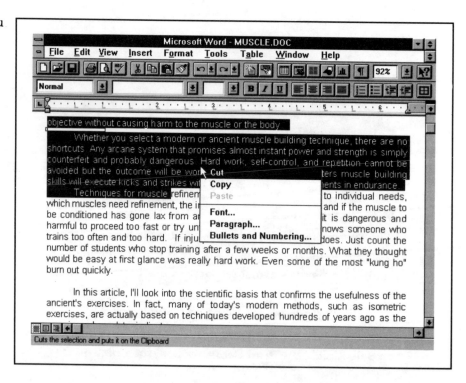

To delete sections of text:

1 Select the text you wish to delete.

2 Press Del or point to the selected text and click the *right* mouse to display the Shortcut Quick menu shown in the figure, then select Cut.

arning! ▷   **Quick delete**

Click on the Cut button to delete selected text.

for more... ▷   **So many choices**

Press Ctrl+Backspace to delete from the insertion point to the beginning of the word; press Ctrl+Del to delete from the insertion point to the end of the word. After selecting text, you can also delete it by selecting Edit ➤ Cut, pressing Ctrl+X, or selecting Edit ➤ Clear.

▲ ▲ ▲ ▲ ▲ ▲

▼ ▼ ▼ ▼ ▼

USING UNDO AND REDO

If you erase text by mistake, you can restore it without retyping. Word remembers all of the editing you perform during a session, so you can "undo" almost every action you perform. If you undo an action, then change your mind again, you can instantly "redo" it.

To undo an action:

❙ Pull down the Undo button in the Standard Toolbar. A list of your actions will be displayed. The item at the top of the list is the last action you performed.

Undo button

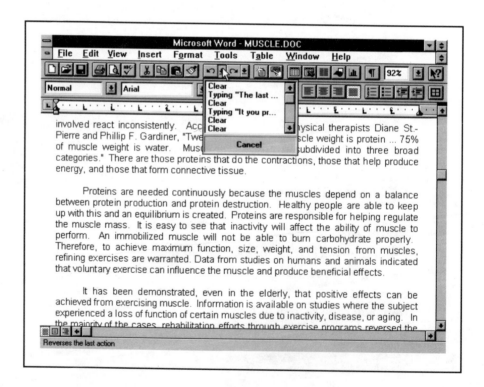

2 Click on the item you want to undo.

3 If you change your mind after undoing the item, pull down the Redo button. A list of your previous undos will be listed. Click on the item you want to redo.

tip ▶ **Simple Undo**
You can also undo actions by selecting Edit ➤ Undo (Ctrl+Z). Do this multiple times to undo multiple actions.

arning! ▶ **Redo**

You can use the Redo button to undo actions of the Edit ➤ Undo command.

oops! ▶ **Be careful!**
The undo list will show the first characters of text to be un-done. To delete text you typed, scroll the list until you see the word Typing followed by the first word or two of the text you want to delete.

▲ ▲ ▲ ▲ ▲ ▲

SEARCHING FOR TEXT

If you spend a lot of time scrolling through documents looking for a particular word or phrase, you can save time by using Word's Find feature. Word can search an entire document for a specific set of characters in seconds.

To locate specific text:

1 Move the insertion point to the location where you want the search to begin. To search the entire document, press Ctrl+Home before searching.

2 Select Edit ➤ Find (Ctrl+F) to display the Find dialog box shown in the figure.

Find dialog box

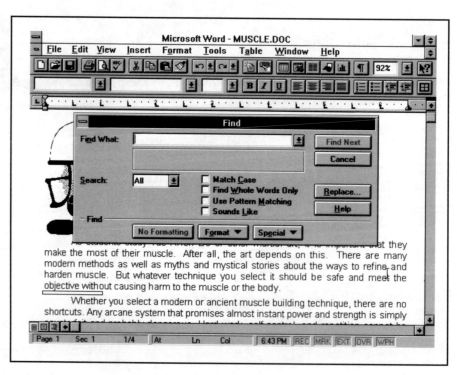

3 Type the characters you want to locate.

4 Press Enter or select Find Next to begin the search.

Word will highlight the next occurrence of the text. The Find dialog box remains on the screen after Word locates the text. To find the next occurrence of the same text, select Find Next.

If the text is not found, a dialog box appears with the message that the search item was not found. Select OK or press Enter to remove the message—the insertion point will be in its original position.

tip ▶ **Search options**

Select Find *Whole Words Only* to locate only entire words that match the search text, not just the characters themselves; *Match Case* to match the case of the characters as you enter them in the Find dialog box; *Sounds Like* to search for words that sound like the text; *Use Pattern Matching* to include the * and ? wild cards in the search text.

tip ▶ **Search for codes**

To locate a formatting code, pull down for format button, select Font, Paragraph, Language, or Style, then select the format. To locate a style such as bold or italic, click on the style's button in the Toolbar.

▲ ▲ ▲ ▲ ▲ ▲ ▲

▼ ▼ ▼ ▼ ▼

REPLACING TEXT AUTOMATICALLY

Have you ever misspelled the same word several times in one document or realized that you entered the wrong information in several places?

In situations like this, you can use the Replace command to automatically locate any text and replace it with something else.

To replace text automatically:

| Move the insertion point to the location where you want the replacements to begin.

Replace dialog box

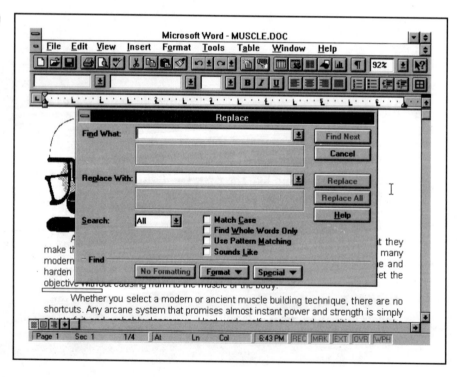

2 Select Edit ➤ Replace (Ctrl+H) to display the Replace dialog box. You can also select Replace from the Find dialog box.

3 Type the text you wish to replace, then press Tab.

4 Type the text you want to insert.

5 Select Replace All.

6 A dialog box will appear, reporting that all matching text has been replaced. Select OK to remove the message, then close the Replace dialog box.

oops! ▶ **Where did it all go?**

Don't forget a Replace With entry. If you leave the entry blank, Word will *delete* the text it locates. If you do this accidentally, select Undo in the Toolbar, then Replace All to restore the text.

tip ▶ **Additional replacement options**

Select *Find Next* to locate the next occurrence of the text without changing it. Select *Replace* to replace the text and locate the next occurrence. Select a search direction in the Search list.

▲ ▲ ▲ ▲ ▲ ▲

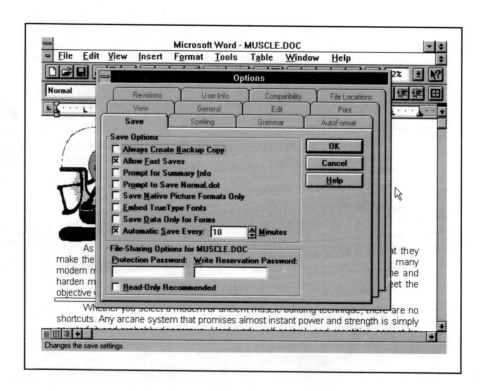

SAVING EDITED TEXT AND BACKUP COPIES

When you save a document for the first time, you have to enter its name in the Save As dialog box. To save it again after making changes, select File ➤ Save or click on the Save button in the Toolbar. The Save As dialog box will not appear, and the file will be saved immediately.

If you want to use the Save command but keep the original version on the disk unchanged, set Word to make backup copies. Then when you save a document, Word gives the original copy the extension .BAK and saves the new version with same name.

Save Options dialog box

In addition, as you work, Word automatically makes a different type of backup copy, called an Automatic Save. Every 10 minutes Word saves a temporary copy of your document. If your machine goes haywire before you save your document, you'll be able to restore your work the next time you start Word.

To change backup options:

1   Select File ➤ Save As ➤ Options to display the dialog box shown in the figure.

2   Select Always Create Backup Copies to make backup copies when you save a document.

3   Click on the Automatic Save option to turn off this feature, or change the time period for saving your work.

4   Select OK then Close to return to the document.

tip ▶ **Don't rely on Automatic Saves**

You must still save your document before exiting Word even if an Automatic Save has just occurred. The Automatic Save document is deleted when you save the document or exit Word. If someone accidentally turns off your computer while you are working in Word, however, the temporary file will remain on the disk. The next time you start Word, the documents in the automatic save files will be opened and displayed on screen with the word Recovered in the Title Bar.

It's So Easy

▶ Moving, Copying, and Automating Text

Selecting text gives you the ability to work with sections of your document as a block. You already know how to delete and print selected portions of a document. In this lesson, you'll learn how to move and copy portions of text, and how to streamline entering text using some special Word features.

▶ ▶ ▶ ▶ ▶ ▶ ▶ ▶

▼ ▼ ▼ ▼ ▼

MOVING TEXT WITH THE MOUSE

When you *move* text, you delete it from one location in a document and place it at another. The quickest way to move text is by using the mouse to *drag and drop*. This means you drag the text to where you want it to appear, then drop it in its new location.

To move text by drag and drop:

1 Select the text you want to move.

2 Place the mouse pointer on the selected text, then press and hold down the left mouse button.

Text ready to be moved with drag and drop

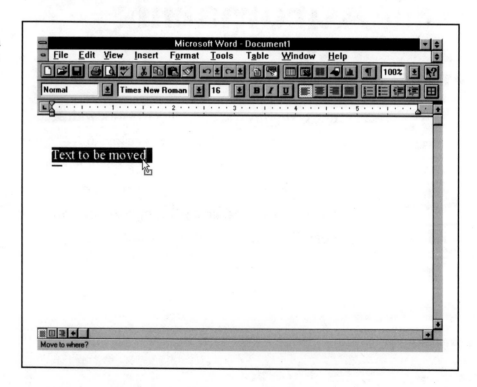

3 Drag the mouse pointer to the location where you want to insert the text. The screen will scroll if you move the pointer to the top or bottom of the screen.

4 Release the mouse button.

oops! ▷ **Change your mind?**
The text isn't actually moved until you release the mouse button. If you decide not to move the text after you begin dragging the mouse, move the pointer back onto the selected text, then release the mouse. If you change you mind after releasing the mouse, select Edit ➤ Undo (Ctrl+Z).

for more... ▷ **Moving to other documents**
To move text to another document, see "Moving Text Between Documents" in Lesson 7.

▲ ▲ ▲ ▲ ▲ ▲

COPYING TEXT WITH THE MOUSE

When you *copy* text, you are really inserting a duplicate of it at another location. The original text is not deleted from the document. You can copy text using drag and drop, in a procedure almost identical to moving text. The only difference is that you use the Ctrl key.

To copy text by drag and drop:

| Select the text you want to copy.

Text ready to be copied with drag and drop

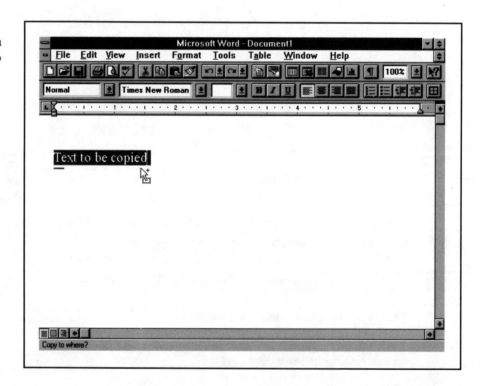

2 Place the mouse pointer on the selected text, then press and hold down the left mouse button.

3 Drag the mouse point to the location where you want to insert the text.

4 Press and hold down the Ctrl key.

5 Release the mouse button.

tip ▶ **Copy or move?**
Press the Ctrl key to copy the text. If you decide to move, rather than copy, the text, release the Ctrl key *before* releasing the mouse button. If you decide not to copy the text after all, release the mouse button then select Edit ➤ Undo (Ctrl+Z).

for more... ▶ **Copying to other documents**
To copy text to another document, see "Moving Text Between Documents" in Lesson 7.

▲ ▲ ▲ ▲ ▲ ▲

MOVING TEXT
WITH CUT AND PASTE

While drag and drop is convenient, you may want to move text using the Cut and Paste commands instead. You'll need to use Cut and Paste to move text between document windows that are not displayed simultaneously.

To Cut and Paste text:

❙ Select the text you want to move.

Shortcut menu
displayed when
text is not
selected

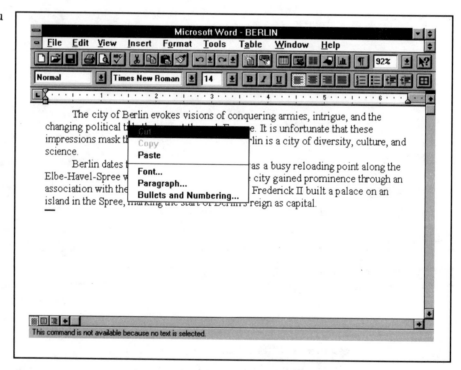

2 Click the *right* mouse button to display the Shortcut menu, then select Cut. The text disappears from the screen. You can also select Edit ➤ Cut (or press Ctrl+X).

3 Position the insertion point where you want to place the text. If you decide not to move the text, place the insertion point at its original location.

4 Click the *right* mouse button to display the Shortcut menu shown in the figure and select Paste.

You can also insert the text by selecting Edit ➤ Paste, or pressing Ctrl+V.

warning! ▶ **Click to Cut and Paste**

Click on the Cut button to delete the text, then click on the Paste button to insert it.

oops! ▶ **I didn't want to do that!**

When you cut or copy text, it replaces whatever is already in the clipboard. If you accidentally cut or copy text, select Edit ➤ Undo.

new feature ▶ **Right button = Shortcut**

The Shortcut menus displayed by pressing the right mouse button are excellent time savers.

▲ ▲ ▲ ▲ ▲ ▲

COPYING TEXT
WITH COPY AND PASTE

You can also copy text from the Shortcut menu or the Edit menu.
The original text is not deleted from the document. You can copy
as much text as you want, and as many times as you want.

To Copy and Paste text:

❙ Select the text you want to copy.

Edit menu with
Copy option
available

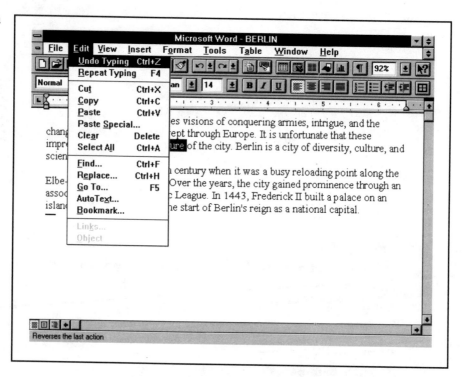

2 Click the *right* mouse button to display the Quick menu, then select Copy, or select Edit ➤ Copy (Ctrl+C).

3 Position the insertion point where you want to place a duplicate of the text.

4 Click the *right* mouse button to display the Quick menu and select Paste.

warning! ▷ **Click to Copy and Paste**

Click on the Copy button to place a copy of the text into the clipboard, then click on the Paste button to insert it. Select Edit ➤ Paste or press Ctrl+V.

tip ▷ **Making multiple copies**

To insert another copy of the text at some other location, move the insertion point, then select Edit ➤ Paste (or press Ctrl+U) again.

▲ ▲ ▲ ▲ ▲ ▲

SAVING TIME
WITH AUTOCORRECT

AutoCorrect watches what you type, correcting common mistakes on the fly. If you accidentally capitalize the first two characters of a word, Word automatically changes the second letter to lowercase. If you transpose the word *and*, typing *adn*, Word automatically corrects it.

You can also add your own AutoCorrect entries to correct words that you frequently misspell, or to insert words and phrases by typing an abbreviation.

AutoCorrect
dialog box

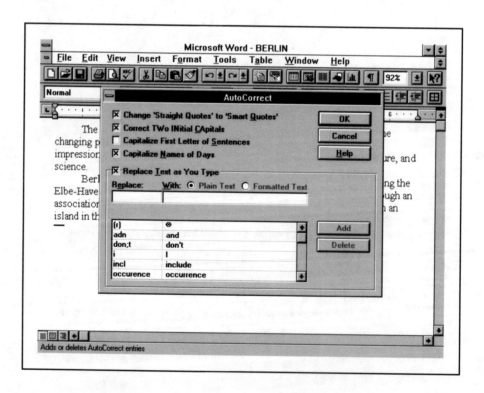

1 Select Tools ➤ AutoCorrect to display the dialog box shown in the figure.

2 In the Replace box, type the way you normally misspell a word, or type an abbreviation for an automatic entry.

3 In the With box, type the correct spelling of the word, or the full text you want displayed with the abbreviation.

4 Select Add, then Close.

To use an AutoCorrect entry:

▶ Type the abbreviation then press the spacebar—the full text will appear. If you misspell the word as specified, the correct word will appear.

tip ▶ **AutoCorrect options**
Use the options in the AutoCorrect to customize this feature: Change 'Straight Quotes' to 'Smart Quotes,' Correct TWo INitial CAptials, Capitalize First Letter of Sentences, Capitalize Names of Days, Replace text as You Type, and Delete.

▲ ▲ ▲ ▲ ▲ ▲

INSERTING TEXT WITH AUTOTEXT

Sometimes you may not want to automatically insert text for an abbreviation. Suppose you enter the AutoCorrect entry Carbon when you type C. The problem is that when writing an outline, the level C will be replaced by the word Carbon. Instead of turning off AutoCorrect, use AutoText. Rather than replace words automatically, you have to press a key, or click a button, to make the replacement.

AutoText
dialog box

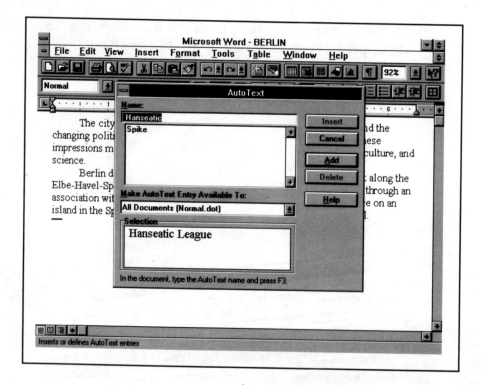

To create an AutoText entry:

1 Type and select the text you want to store as AutoText.

2 Select Edit ➤ AutoText. Use the entry in the Name box to insert the text into your documents.

3 Select Add to accept the name, or type another identifying name for the text then select Add.

To insert an AutoText entry:

▶ Type the entry name, then press F3.

power bar **Use the button**

When text is selected, click on the AutoText button to display the AutoText dialog box. To insert an entry, type the name then click on the AutoText button. If you hear a beep, AutoText cannot identify the name.

tip ▶ **Abbreviate**

You do not have to type the complete AutoText name, just enough characters to identify the entry. For example, if you have only one AutoText entry that starts with the letter B, just type B and then press F3.

▲ ▲ ▲ ▲ ▲ ▲

▼ ▼ ▼ ▼ ▼

USING THE SPIKE

There are times when you may want to cut or copy a number of sections of text, collect them into a group, then insert them together at one location. You cannot use the clipboard since the contents are replaced when you cut or copy another selection. Instead, use the Spike. Adding text to the Spike does not erase its contents—the new text is appended to whatever is already there.

To add text to the Spike:

▶ Select the text and press Ctrl+F3.

Spike entry selected in the AutoText dialog box

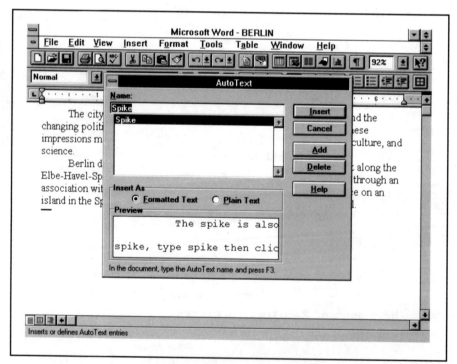

To insert the contents of the Spike in the document:

▶ Place the insertion point where you want to insert the text, type **spike**, then press F3.

To insert the contents and empty the Spike:

▶ Place the insertion point where you want to insert the text, type **spike**, then press Ctrl+Shift+F3.

Fine-Tuning Your Documents

The editing techniques you've learned so far are sufficient for most simple editing, but you'll also want to take advantage of Word's comprehensive array of special editing capabilities. You may not use the techniques you'll learn in this lesson for every short note you write, but they are invaluable for fine-tuning your documents.

DISPLAYING FORMAT CHARACTERS

Keys such as Tab and Enter do not display any characters on the screen, but they do insert invisible characters that affect the format of the text. Revealing these characters makes it easy to correct formatting errors, such as extra spaces between words and sentences.

To display formatting characters:

▶ Click on the Show/Hide button in the Standard Toolbar— the button with the ¶ symbol.

Word screen showing format characters

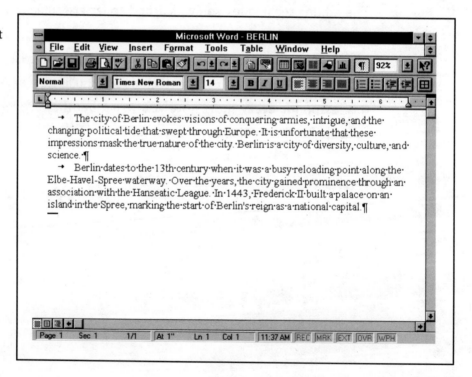

Your screen will look much like the figure on the facing page. Spaces are indicated by bullets; tabs by the →; and hard returns inserted by pressing Enter by the ¶ symbol.

To remove the display, click on the button again.

tip ▶ **Working with codes**

If you want, you can leave the characters revealed as you write.

tip ▶ **Fine tuning**

Display the characters before printing an important document. Look for extra spaces between words (two consecutive bullets) or sentences you indented by typing spaces rather than pressing tab. Using spaces may result in incorrect alignment with certain fonts.

▲ ▲ ▲ ▲ ▲ ▲

▶ ▶ ▶

▼ ▼ ▼ ▼ ▼

INSERTING THE DATE

We use the date in letters and many other documents. You can have Word insert the correct date automatically as either *text* or as a *field*. When you insert the date as text, the current date is inserted into the document just as if you typed it yourself.

When you insert the date as a field, the current date will be inserted just as if you had entered it as text, but will change to the current date if you open or print the document some other day.

To insert the date:

❙ Select Insert ➤ Date and Time to see the dialog box shown in the figure.

Date and Time
dialog box

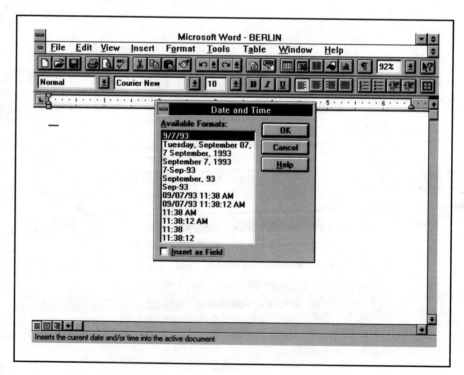

◄ ◄ ◄

2 Select the format you want the date to appear in.

3 To insert the date as a field, select Insert as Field.

4 To insert the date as text, make sure the Insert as Field box is cleared.

5 Click on OK.

You can press Alt+Shift+D to insert the date as text, and Alt+Shift+T to insert the time.

tip ▶ **Erasing the date field**
When you enter the date as a field, the date appears on screen but it is stored as a single code in the document. To erase the date, select it and press Del. You cannot delete it by pressing Del or Backspace when it is not selected.

tip ▶ **Updating the date or time**
When you enter the date and time as a field, it will be updated when you open the document. To update it manually, select the date or time, and then press F9.

▲ ▲ ▲ ▲ ▲ ▲

▼ ▼ ▼ ▼ ▼

REPEATING KEYSTROKES

Sometimes you'll want to repeat a certain word or phrase, or to perform some editing action more than once. For example, you may type a phrase, then want to insert it in another location.

You can use the Repeat command to perform repeated actions easily and quickly. To repeat your last typing or action:

1 Place the insertion point where you want to begin repeating.

2 Select Edit ➤ Repeat, or press F4.

Edit menu showing Repeat options

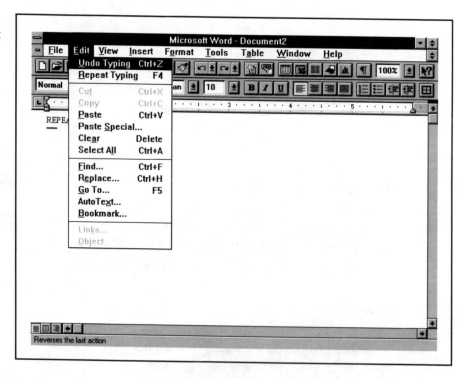

If you just typed something, the same text will appear at the location of the insertion point. If you just deleted a word, the word at the insertion point will be deleted.

tip ▶ **Reading the menu**
The full name of the Repeat command in the Edit menu depends on the last action that you performed. For example, it may appear as Repeat Typing, Repeat Cut, Repeat Page Break, Repeat Formatting, etc. If Word cannot repeat your last action, it will appear dimmed as Can't Repeat.

oops! ▶ **Hearing bells**
Word will sound a beep if it cannot repeat an action when you press F4.

▲ ▲ ▲ ▲ ▲ ▲

INSERTING PAGE BREAKS

As you type, Word will divide your document into pages automatically. When a new page starts, a dotted line appears across the screen and the Page indicator in the Status Bar increases by one. (In Page Layout view, page break lines are two-tone.) Automatic page breaks are called *soft page breaks*. The position of a soft page break can change as you insert or delete text.

Break dialog box with document showing two hard page breaks in the background

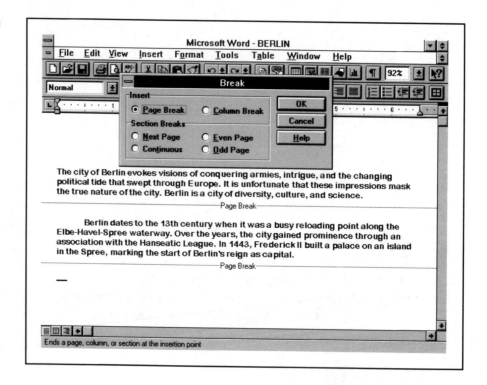

There may be times, however, when you'll want to end a page yourself—such as for a short memo or title page. This is called a *hard page break*. A hard page break is a dotted line with the words Page Break in the center of the screen.

To insert a hard page break:

▶ Press Ctrl+Enter or select Insert ➤ Break ➤ OK.

Word will insert a line like the ones shown in the figure.

oops! ▶ **Beware of redundant page breaks**

If you add enough text above a hard page break, Word may insert a soft page break when the page becomes full. When you print the document, you'll end up with a blank page between the soft and hard page breaks. Before printing a document, scroll through it to check the position of page breaks.

tip ▶ **Deleting hard page breaks**

Place the insertion point on the page break line and press Del.

CREATING A TEMPLATE

Suppose you have a document that contains just the headings for a memo. You open the document and type the specifics of the memo in the appropriate locations. However, if you save the document without changing the name, it will now contain the text of an actual memo, not just the headings. The next time you want to type a memo, you have to retype the headings in a new document.

A Word template is a special type of document that contains only standard text and formats. Once you create a template, you can open it to enter text but you must save it with a different name. The original template will remain unchanged unless you specifically want to edit it.

New dialog box listing templates

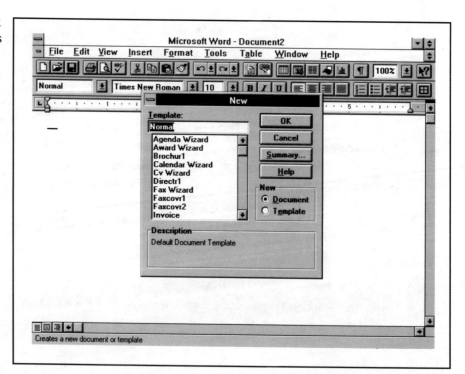

◀ ◀ ◀

To create a template:

1 Select File ➤ New to display the dialog box shown in the figure.

2 Click on the Template radio button.

3 Select OK.

4 Type the standard text that you want in the template, then select File ➤ Save.

5 Enter a name for the template and then select OK. Word saves templates with the DOT extension.

6 Select File ➤ Close.

tip ▶ **Editing a template**
Select File ➤ Open, select Template in the Directories list, pull down the List Files of Type box, and select Document Templates (*.dot). Double click on the template you want to edit, make your changes, then select File ➤ Save.

arning! ▶ **Do not use the button**

Clicking on the New button in the Toolbar opens a new document using the standard template—the template that contains Word's default settings. It does *not* display the Template dialog box.

▲ ▲ ▲ ▲ ▲ ▲

▼   ▼   ▼   ▼   ▼

USING A TEMPLATE

When you want to type a document using a template, start a new document using the template as its pattern. Word opens the template into a blank new document window. Add the specific text you want, then save the document with a new name. Because the template is opened in a new document window, selecting File ➤ Save will not overwrite the template with the edited document.

Word's
FaxCovr2
template

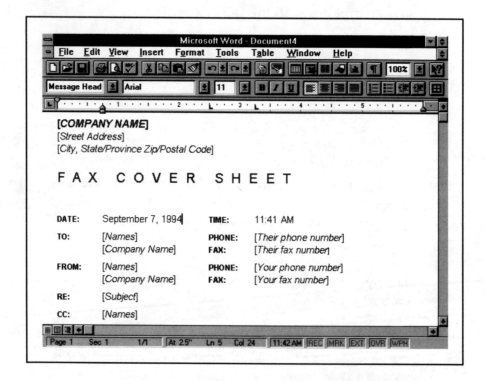

To use a template:

1 Select File ➤ New to display the Template dialog box.

2 Double-click on the template you want to use, or select the template and click on OK.

3 Type the specific text for the document.

4 Select File ➤ Save As, enter a document name, then select OK.

for more... ▶ **Word templates**

Word provides a number of useful templates to get you started. The Template box also lists a number of document Wizards. You'll learn how to use the Wizards later in this Lesson.

new feature ▶ **Standard letters**

Word provides samples of standard business letters in the **WINWORD\LETTERS** directory. Open a letter (with the .dot extension) and edit it to fit your needs.

▲ ▲ ▲ ▲ ▲ ▲

USING WIZARDS

A Wizard is similar to a template, except Word prompts you for the necessary information, and inserts it automatically in the document. For fax cover pages and other documents, Word can even use the name and company that you inserted when you installed Word.

To use a Wizard:

❙ Select File ➤ New to display the Template dialog box.

Initial dialog box for the CV Wizard

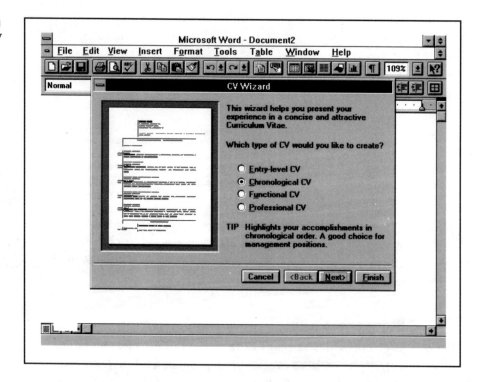

2 Double-click on the Wizard you want to use, or select the template then click on OK. The names of Wizards indicate the show the type of document, followed by the word Wizard.

3 A prompt in the Status Bar will ask you to insert information, or one or more dialog boxes will appear requesting formatting choices or text to insert into the document.

4 Enter the information requested in the prompts.

If a dialog box is displayed, select Options from the box, or enter text in text boxes, then select Next> to move to the next box. Select Finish after completing the final dialog box. The document will appear formatted as you selected and containing the text entered.

tip ▶ **Other options**
In Wizard dialog boxes, select Cancel to stop the procedure, or select <Back to return to the previous dialog box in the series.

tip ▶ **Watch that status line**
Before the first dialog box appears, Word may have to set up the format, load a file, or perform another operation. Watch the Status line for a report on Word's progress.

It's So Easy

▶ Using Multiple Documents and Windows

With Word, you can open and work on several documents at the same time. Say you're typing a report and
you need to refer back to a document you typed last week.
Instead of looking for a printout of the document, you
can open it in its own window and refer to it while you
are typing your current report.

You can also display two parts of the document, or display it in two views at the same time, using panes. One pane
could display the document in outline or Page Layout
view, the other pane in Normal view.

In this lesson, you'll learn how to best take advantage
of Word windows and panes.

DIVIDING A
DOCUMENT INTO PANES

Sometimes you need to refer to one section of a document while you are writing or editing another section. You may also need to move or copy text from one location in a document to another. Rather than scroll the document back and forth, divide the screen into two panes. You can display two different sections of the document in the panes in different views—if you want—and drag and drop text from one pane to the other.

To create panes:

❙ Select Window ➤ Split. A line appears across the screen.

Document
split into panes

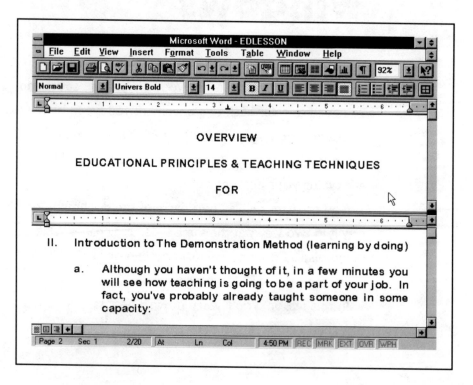

2 Drag the line, or press the up or down arrows, to position the split where you want it.

3 Release the mouse button, or press Enter if you are using the keyboard.

If the Ruler is displayed, a second Ruler Bar appears across the screen at the split position.

tip ▶ **Using the mouse**
You can also split the window using the Split box, the black rectangle above the Scroll Bar. Drag the Split box to the desired split location.

tip ▶ **Unsplitting a window**
To remove the split, select Window ➤ Unsplit, or drag the Split box off the bottom of the screen.

for more... ▶ **One document, multiple windows**
If you want to display a document in more than two views, open the document into multiple windows rather than split it into panes. Each time you select Window ➤ New, Word opens another window containing the same document, adding the notation :2, :3, and so forth to the Title Bar.

▲ ▲ ▲ ▲ ▲ ▲

▼　▼　▼　▼　▼

WORKING WITH PANES

When you split a window, both panes have their own Ruler Bar and Scroll Bars. You can scroll each pane independently to display two different sections of the same document. However, changes you make in one pane may affect the document in the other pane. The active pane is the one which contains the insertion point.

To select a pane:

▶ Click in the pane with the mouse or press F6 to move from pane to pane.

A split document showing two views and zoom of the same section of text

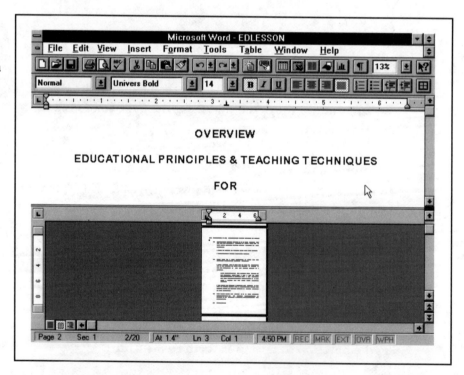

To scroll a pane:

▶ Select the pane, then use the scroll bar in that pane.

To change the view or magnification of a pane:

▶ Select the pane, then change the view or zoom settings.

new feature ▶ **Moving text between panes**
To move or copy text from one pane to another, use drag and drop. Select the text in one pane, then drag it to the desired position in the other pane, then release the mouse button. Hold down the Ctrl key to copy the text. You can also use Cut and Paste or Copy and Paste.

for more... ▶ **In pane view**
Displaying a whole page in Page Layout view is useful for seeing the overall layout of the page, but you cannot read the text. Split the document into panes; use Normal view in one pane, Page Layout in zoomed to Whole Page in the other, as shown in the Figure. Changes you make to the text and layout in the Normal view pane will automatically be reflected in the whole page display.

OPENING
MULTIPLE DOCUMENTS

Working with multiple documents vastly increases your productivity and efficiency. You can write or edit one document while using others for reference. When you open a second document, the first one is not erased—it is just moved into the background. When you open multiple documents, each appears in its own window.

Several documents selected for opening

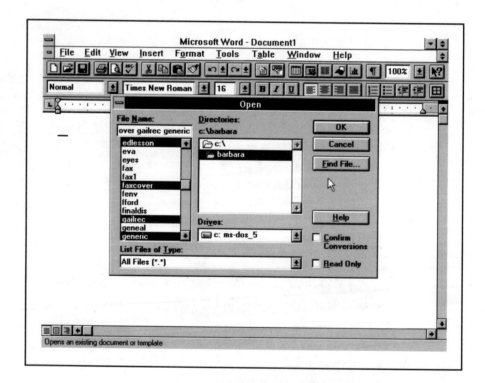

To open another document, do one of the following:

▸ When one document is on the screen, use File ➤ Open or the open button in the Toolbar to open another.

▸ Select File ➤ New to open a blank document window to type a new document.

To open several documents at one time:

1 Select File ➤ Open.

2 Hold down the Ctrl key and click on each of the documents you want to open.

3 Click on OK.

tip ▶ **Combining documents**
To insert the text of a file on disk into the displayed document, place the insertion point where you want the file to appear, and select Insert ➤ File. Then, select the file to insert from the File Name list, then select **OK**.

tip ▶ **Windows, not panes**
The windows are totally independent: scrolling or editing in one window does not effect any other window.

SWITCHING BETWEEN DOCUMENTS

While you can have multiple documents open at a time, only one is active. That is, you can only actually edit or format one document at a time. However, you can quickly switch from document to document.

To switch between documents, do one of the following:

▶ Pull down the Window menu and click on the name of the document you want to display from the list of open documents.

Window menu

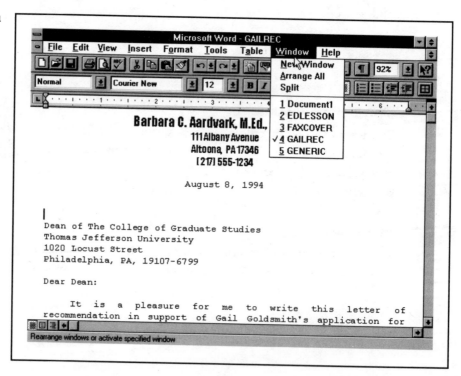

▶ Press Ctrl+F6.

When you switch back to a document, the position of the insertion point will be right where you left it.

tip ▶ **Independent windows**
Changing views (from **Normal** to **Page Layout**, for example) or magnification in one document will not affect the view of the other documents.

tip ▶ **Prying eyes?**
If you have a document whose contents you'd rather not share with others in your office, try this trick. Click on the **New** button in the **Toolbar** to open a blank window, then press **Ctrl+F6** to select your document window. If someone who should not see your work approaches, press **Ctrl+F6** to display the blank window.

▲ ▲ ▲ ▲ ▲ ▲

▼ ▼ ▼ ▼ ▼

DISPLAYING MULTIPLE WINDOWS

If you are working on several complex documents, you can move and copy text between them more efficiently if you display all of them on the screen at one time. You can divide the screen into multiple windows, and move from window to window using the mouse or keyboard.

To display multiple windows:

▶ Select Window ➤ Arrange All.

Tiled windows

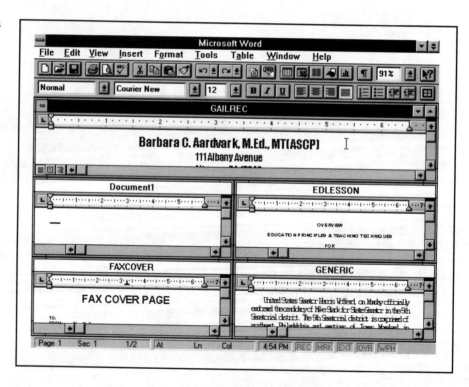

The windows will become tiled, which means that Word reduces the size of the document windows so they fill the screen without overlapping.

To switch between displayed windows:

► Click on the window you want to make active. You can also press Ctrl+F6.

tip ▶ **Overlapping windows**

If you open other documents while the windows are tiled, the new windows are cascaded—displayed overlapping each other and the tiled windows. When windows overlap, making one active will bring it into the foreground.

tip ▶ **Telling active from inactive**

Only one document window can be active at a time. The Title Bars of inactive windows are white; the Title Bar of the displayed window is blue (or in reverse in black and white displays).

▲ ▲ ▲ ▲ ▲ ▲

CHANGING THE SIZE AND POSITION OF WINDOWS

You can quickly make the active window full-size by maximizing it, or change it to an icon by minimizing it. You can also customize the size and position of windows using the mouse.

To change the size of a window:

▶ Drag one of the corners to change both the height and width of a window at one time.

Windows
moved
side-by-side

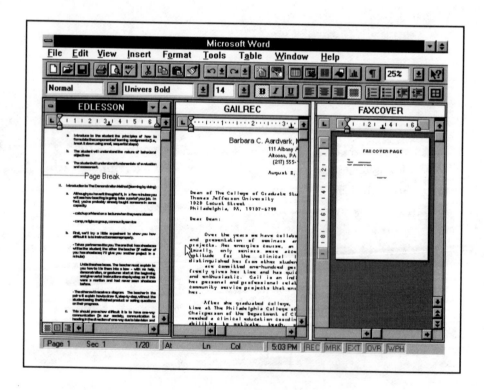

▶ Drag the left or right border to change the width.

▶ Drag the top or bottom border to change the height.

To move a window:

▶ Point to the Title Bar and drag the mouse in the direction you want to move the window.

tip ▶   **Getting the correct size and position**

As you drag the mouse, an outline of the window moves along with it. When the outline is the size you want, or in the correct position, release the mouse button. You can not move a window beyond the edge of the screen.

▲ ▲ ▲ ▲ ▲ ▲

MOVING TEXT BETWEEN DOCUMENTS

You can move and copy text from one open document to another—whether or not they are displayed at the same time. The techniques are the same as those explained in Lesson 5. You can drag and drop text from one window to another.

To move or copy text between displayed documents:

▶ Drag and drop the text from one window to the other.

Text about to be copied from one document to another

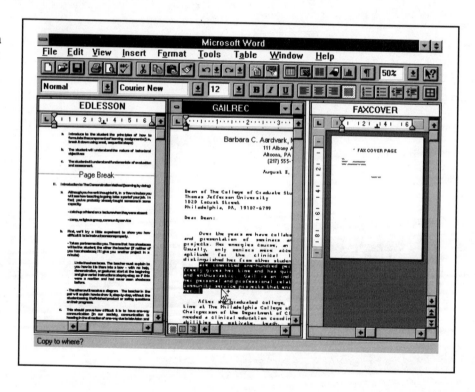

To move or copy text between overlapped windows:

1 Select the text you want to move or copy.

2 Select Edit ➤ Cut to move text, deleting it from its original document; or select Edit ➤ Copy to insert a duplicate of the text in another document.

3 Switch to the document you want to place the text in, or select File ➤ New to insert it into a new document.

4 Select Edit ➤ Paste or click on the Paste button in the Toolbar.

warning! ▶

Shortcuts

You can use the Cut, Copy, and Paste buttons on the Toolbar instead of using the Edit menu. You can also click the right mouse button and select Cut, Copy, or Paste from the Shortcut menu.

tip ▶ **Moving text to unopened documents**

You can move and copy text from an open document to one not yet opened. Select the text you want to cut or copy, then select Edit ➤ Cut or Edit ➤ Copy. Open the other document, then select Edit ➤ Paste. Before opening the other document, you can also close the first.

▲ ▲ ▲ ▲ ▲ ▲ ▲

PART TWO ▶ **Exercises**

You now know how easy it is to edit a document using Word. Let's practice your new editing skills.

Opening Documents

We'll start by creating and saving a small document. Then, we'll practice opening the document using the File menu and the Open dialog box.

1 Start Windows and Word for Windows.

2 Press Tab and type the following text:

> **Marriage is a civil contract between two individuals. Unlike other civil contracts, the marriage contract cannot be terminated simply by obtaining the consent of both parties. The contract can only be terminated by a judicial decree, or by the death of one of the parties. A marriage contract can be declared void, however, upon proof of fraud or incompetence of one of the parties, or if one of the parties is found to be underage.**

3 Select File ➤ Save (Ctrl+S), type **MARRIAGE**, then select OK.

4 Select File ➤ Close to clear the window.

Now let's practice opening the document.

5 Select File. MARRIAGE.DOC is listed at the bottom of the File menu.

6 Click on the file name, MARRIAGE.DOC, or press the number listed next to the file name. When you open a document, the insertion point is automatically at the top of the page.

7 Select File ➤ Close to clear the window.

Now let's use the Open dialog box.

8 Select File ➤ Open, or click on the Open button in the Toolbar. A list of files in the default directory appears.

9 Double-click on MARRIAGE.DOC (scroll the list, if necessary). You can also highlight the document name, then click on OK.

10 Select File ➤ Close to clear the window.

11 Select File ➤ Exit if you're not ready to go on.

Inserting, Selecting and Editing Text

Now let's add some text to the document, then practice selecting text and using the Undo command.

1 Open MARRIAGE.DOC if it is not already on your screen.

2 Place the insertion point at the end of the last sentence in the document.

3 Press Enter twice to insert a blank line.

4 Press Tab to indent the paragraph, then type the following:

> **The legal age at which an individual can enter into a marriage contract varies among the states. In addition, every state requires the parties to obtain a marriage license, and the states may impose restrictions if they see fit.**

5 Place the insertion point in front of the first paragraph.

6 Hold down the left mouse button, then drag the mouse to the end of the paragraph. If you're not using the mouse, position the insertion point, press F8, then use the ↓ and → to select the text.

7 Press Del. Oops! We really don't want to delete all that text.

8 Select Edit ➤ Undo Clear (Ctrl+Z) to restore the deleted text.

9 Click the mouse, or move the insertion point, to deselect the text.

10 Place the insertion point before the period at the end of the third sentence in the first paragraph, the sentence ending with the phrase *by the death of one of the parties*.

11 Press the spacebar to insert a space.

12 Type **including when caused by the surviving party.** Well, we didn't want to give anyone any ideas.

13 Select Edit ➤ Undo Typing (Ctrl+Z) to delete the text.

14 Click on the Save button in the Toolbar, or select File ➤
Save. Since the document already has a name, it is saved
immediately.

15 Select File ➤ Exit if you're not ready to go on.

Moving and Copying Text

It's time to move and copy text. We'll start by copying text to
make a title.

1 Open MARRIAGE.DOC if it is not already on your screen.

2 Place the insertion point at the start of the document, at the
far left in front of the first paragraph.

3 Press Enter twice to insert two blank lines.

4 Select the word Marriage in the first paragraph.

5 Place the mouse pointer on the selected word, hold down the
left mouse button (do not release it until after the next step),
then drag the pointer to the top of the document, in the first
blank line. Do not release the mouse button yet.

6 Hold down the Ctrl key, release the mouse button, then release the Ctrl key. If you do not have a mouse, select the text,
then select Edit ➤ Copy. Move the insertion point to the top
of the document, then select Edit ➤ Paste.

7 Click on the Save button in the Toolbar or select File ➤ Save.
Figure 2.1 shows the completed document.

8 Select File ➤ Exit if you're not ready to go on.

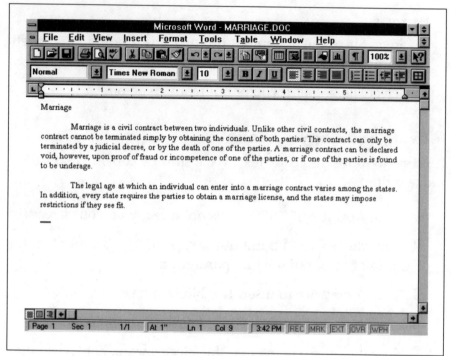

Some Advanced Editing

Let's try the AutoCorrect and AutoText features, and add the date to the document.

1 Open MARRIAGE.DOC if it is not already on your screen.

2 Place the insertion point at the start of the document.

3 Press Enter twice to insert a blank line.

4 Move the insertion point to the top of the document, at the left margin in the blank line.

5 Select Insert ➤ Date and Time, choose the second date format in the list, then select OK.

6 Move the insertion point to the end of the document, and press Enter twice to insert a blank line.

7 Type the following text exactly as shown, including the obvious mistakes, then press Enter:

i don't think i will ever get MArried.

AutoCorrect will automatically correct the text so it appears as

I don't think I will ever get Married

Since the word *contract* is used so often in legal documents, let's add it to the AutoCorrect feature to enter automatically.

8 Select Tools ➤ AutoCorrect.

9 In the Replace text box, type **c**.

10 In the With text box, type **contract**.

11 Select Add, then click OK.

12 Type the following text, using the letter c where you want to insert the word contract:

The c is binding on both parties as long as the c is legally completed.

AutoCorrect will insert the word contract at both occurrences of the letter c. If you enter an uppercase C and then press the spacebar, the word ***contract*** will appear in uppercase.

Now, let's use AutoText to insert the word marriage into the document.

13 Select the word marriage in the second paragraph—double-click on the word.

14 Select Edit ➤ AutoText.

15 In the Name text box, type **mar**, then select Add.

16 Move the insertion point to the end of the document, type **mar** and then press F3 to insert the whole word.

Now, let's delete the AutoCorrect and AutoText entries.

17 Select Tools ➤ AutoCorrect.

18 In the list box, select the line that contains the entry for c and contract, then choose Delete.

19 Click on OK.

20 Select Edit ➤ AutoText. The entry for *mar* should be selected.

21 Click on Delete, then Close.

22 Select File ➤ Close ➤ No to close the document without saving the changes.

23 Select File ➤ Exit if you're not ready to go on.

Working with Wizards

Word's Wizards take you step-by-step through creating awards, agenda, calendars, legal documents, and other common documents. Let's try out the Award Wizard now.

1 Select File ➤ New.

2 Double-click on Award Wizard to display a dialog box of style options, as in Figure 2.2.

3 Click on Decorative to select a style, then choose Next to display a dialog box of paper options.

4 Select Next to accept the default landscape orientation without a preprinted border. A dialog box appears requesting the name of the recipient and the award title.

5 Select the first text box, and type your name.

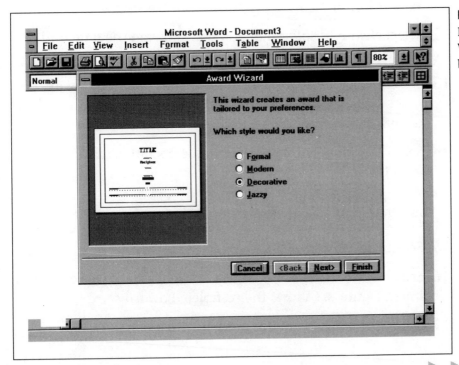

Figure 2.2:
First Award Wizard dialog box

6 Select the second text box, and then type **Employee of the Year**.

7 Select Next to display a dialog box requesting the names of those signing the award.

8 Select the first text box and delete any name that may appear there—if you installed Word, your own name may appear.

9 Type **Bill Clinton**, then select Add.

10 Select Next to display a dialog box and enter the name of the presenting organization.

11 Select Presented By, click in the text box, then type **The World Bank**.

12 Select Next to display a dialog box showing the date and the reason for the award.

13 Select Next to accept the default values. A dialog box appears asking if you want to display help information. The default setting is No.

14 Select Finish. Word will generate the document and display it on the screen.

You can add or edit the text before printing the award.

15 Select File ➤ Print ➤ OK.

16 Select File ➤ Close ➤ No to close the document without saving it. Figure 2.3 shows the completed award.

17 Select File ➤ Exit if you're not ready to go on.

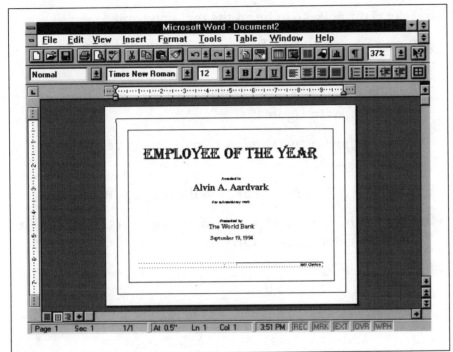

Figure 2.3:
Award created
with Award
Wizard

Working with Windows

Finally, we'll see how to work with more than one document.

1 Open MARRIAGE.DOC.

2 Select the last paragraph in the document.

3 Select Edit ➤ Copy, then deselect the text.

4 Select File ➤ New ➤ OK (or click on the New button) to start a new document.

5 Select Edit ➤ Paste to insert the text you copied.

6 Press Ctrl+F6, or select Window ➤ MARRIAGE.DOC to switch back to the other window.

7 Select Window ➤ Arrange All to display both windows on the screen, as in Figure 2.4.

8 Click on the inactive window to make it active, or press Ctrl+F6.

9 Select File ➤ Close ➤ No to close the active window.

10 Click on the Maximize button on the right of the active window's Title Bar, or press Ctrl+F10.

11 Select File ➤ Exit.

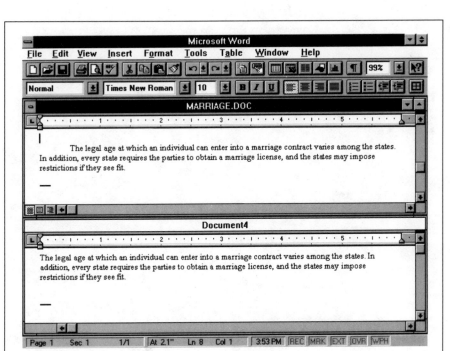

Figure 2.4:
Two windows

**part
three**

FORMATTING
YOUR DOCUMENTS

If a document's appearance wasn't important, we might still be using typewriters. Computers, printers, and programs such as Word let us add impact to even the most routine documents.

In the lessons that follow, you'll learn how to format your documents. After all, it's a tough, competitive world out there. You have to grab the reader's attention and keep it.

It's So Easy

▶ Changing the Appearance of Characters

Word can give your documents a desktop-published, professional look. But don't overdo it! Too many fonts and styles make text more difficult to read and rather unpleasant to the eye.

▶ ▶ ▶ ▶ ▶ ▶ ▶ ▶

▼ ▼ ▼ ▼ ▼

USING BOLD,
UNDERLINE, AND ITALIC

The quickest way to format characters is by using the Toolbar.
The Toolbar contains buttons for bold, italic, and underline.

To format characters:

1 Type until you are ready to format characters.

2 Click on the Toolbar button for the format you want.

▶ Click on the Bold button (or press Ctrl+B) to boldface.

Character
formats

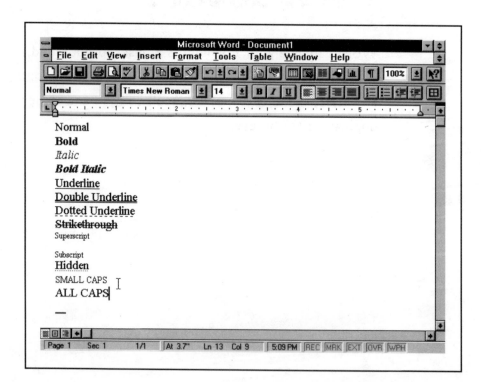

I

▶ Click on the Italic button (or press Ctrl+I) to italicize.

U

▶ Click on the Underline button (or press Ctrl+U) to underline.

3 Type the characters.

4 Select the same style button, or press the Ctrl+key combination again to turn the feature off.

You can also format characters in these and other styles using the Font menu, explained later in this lesson. The screen on the facing page shows the character formats.

tip ▶ **Changing your mind**
To change the appearance of text after typing it, select the text then apply the bold, italic, underline, or any other format. For more information on selecting text, see Lesson 4.

tip ▶ **Removing character formats**
To remove a format from text, select the text, then click the Toolbar button or press the Ctrl-key combination of the format you want to delete. To remove all character formats, select the text and press Ctrl+Spacebar.

▲ ▲ ▲ ▲ ▲ ▲

▶ ▶ ▶

▼ ▼ ▼ ▼ ▼

CHANGING TYPE FONTS AND SIZES WITH THE TOOLBAR

A *font* refers to the general shape or design of the characters. You can select from all of the fonts built into your printer, as well as the TrueType and other scalable fonts installed in Windows.

To change font with the Toolbar:

| Click on the ↓ next to the font name text box to display a list of available fonts.

Font list from the Toolbar

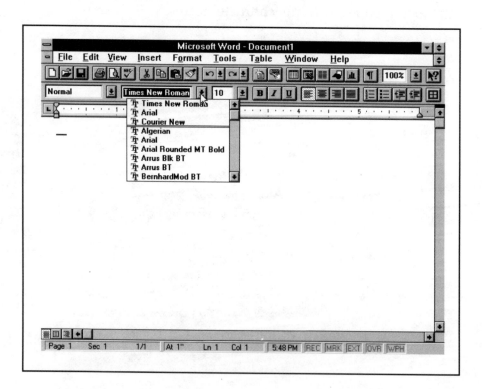

2 Click on the desired font. Scroll the list, if necessary.

To change the size with the Toolbar.

│ 10 │

Ⅰ Click on the ↓ next to the Font Size text box to display a list of point sizes for the selected font.

2 Click on the desired size.

3 Type the text you want in that font and size.

for more... ▶ **Reading the font list**
The available fonts will be listed in alphabetical order. However, the fonts you most recently used will appear at the start of the list, above a double line.

tip ▶ **Changing the font of existing text**
To change the font or size of text you've already typed, select the text first, then select a font and size. To enter a portion of text in a new font, type the text first, select it, then choose the font and size.

▲ ▲ ▲ ▲ ▲ ▲

129

▼ ▼ ▼ ▼ ▼

USING THE
FONT DIALOG BOX

As an alternative to using the Toolbar, you can change character formats, fonts, and sizes with the Font dialog box shown in the figure. The Font dialog box lets you select effects, such as strike-through and small caps, which are not available in the Toolbar.

To change character styles with the dialog box:

▎ Select Format ➤ Font, or click right to display the Shortcut menu, then select Font. Word displays the Font dialog box.

Font dialog box

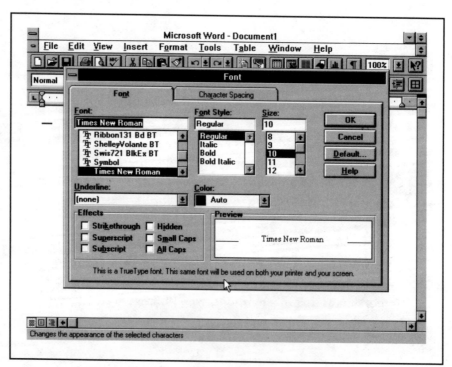

2   Select a font from the Font list.

3   Select a style from the Font Style list.

4   Select the size from the Size list.

5   Select other font attributes or print colors.

6   Select OK.

7   Type the text you want in that font and size.

tip ▶   **Changing the font of existing text**

To change the font or size of text you've already typed, select the text first, then select options from the Font dialog box.

for more... ▶   **Changing the default font**

Word automatically begins each document using a Times Roman font. To change the default font, select a font, style, and size in the Font dialog box, click on Default, then select Yes from the dialog box that appears. The font will be used for all documents using the normal template.

▲ ▲ ▲ ▲ ▲ ▲

CREATING
A DROP CAPITAL

A drop capital is a large initial letter that begins a paragraph. Drop capitals are used in books, annual reports, and other publications to attract the reader's attention.

To have Word create a drop capital:

| Place the insertion point at the start of the paragraph so the letter to appear as the drop capital is to the immediate right of the insertion point.

Drop Cap dialog box with drop capital in the background

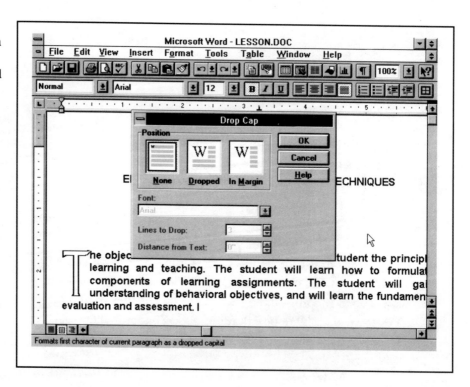

2 Select Format ➤ Drop Cap to display the dialog box shown in the figure.

3 Select either Dropped or In Margin to set the position of the letter.

4 Select a font to use for the character.

5 In the Lines to Drop text box, enter the number of lines high you want the character.

6 Select OK.

7 If you are in Normal view, a dialog box appears asking if you want to change to Page Layout view. Select Yes.

8 Word displays the drop capital in a frame. Click in the document to remove the frame from the display. You'll learn more about frames in Lesson 16.

tip ▶ **Normal view**
In Normal view, the drop capital will appear on a line separate from the text, however the document will print correctly. Change to Page Layout view or Print Preview to see how the Drop Cap appears.

tip ▶ **Drop words**
To drop the entire first word in the paragraph, select the word before choosing Format ➤ Drop Cap.

tip ▶ **To remove a drop capital**
To remove a drop capital, select the letter, then select Format ➤ Drop Cap ➤ None.

▲ ▲ ▲ ▲ ▲ ▲

CHANGING THE CASE OF CHARACTERS

Normally, you enter uppercase characters from the keyboard by pressing the Shift key or the Caps Lock key. But have you ever accidentally pressed Caps Lock, only to notice the mistake after you've typed several paragraphs? Rather than retype the whole thing, you can quickly change the case of existing characters using the Format menu.

To change the case of text:

❙ Select the text you want to change.

Change Case
dialog box

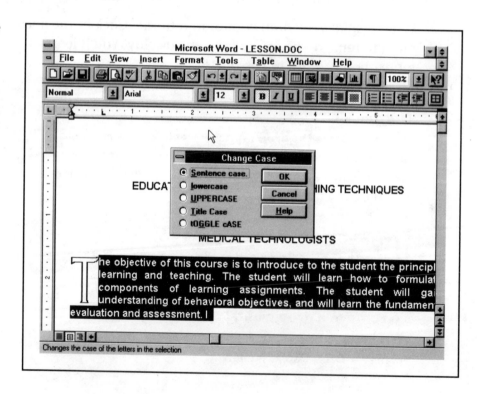

2 Select Format ➤ Change Case.

3 Select one of the following:

▶ **Sentence Case:** Uppercases the first letter of each sentence.

▶ **lowercase:** converts all characters to lowercase.

▶ **UPPERCASE:** converts all characters to uppercase.

▶ **Title Case:** uppercases the first letter of every word.

▶ **tOGGLE cASE:** changes all characters to their opposite case.

oops! ▶ **That's not what I wanted**
If you select a case option by mistake, select Edit ➤ Undo Change Case.

tip ▶ **Lower case**
Selecting lower case will convert *every* character in the sentence, including the first letter in the sentence and the pronoun I.

▲ ▲ ▲ ▲ ▲ ▲

INSERTING SPECIAL CHARACTERS AND SYMBOLS

In this era of international business, it is no longer uncommon to need to print accented characters, and mathematical, scientific, and graphical symbols. With Word, you can easily insert these special characters.

To insert special characters and symbols:

| Select Insert ➤ Symbol to see the dialog box shown in the figure. By default, Word displays the characters available in the current font.

Symbol dialog box with sample characters from the Wingdings font in the background

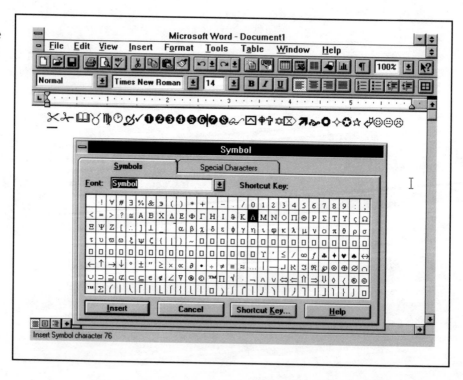

2 Select a font that contains the character you want to insert.

3 Double-click on the symbol you want to insert, or click once on a character to display an enlarged view, then select Insert.

4 Select Close.

The character will appear at the position of the insertion point, in a size to match that of the current font. You can change its size just as you can for any text.

tip ▶ **Selecting fonts**

Most TrueType fonts contain common accented characters and a selection of special symbols. In the Symbol dialog box, pull down the Font list and select the Symbols font to display Greek characters and mathematical symbols. Select Wingdings to insert pictographs, circled numbers, and other special graphics.

for more... ▶ **Inserting special characters**

You can also insert typographical characters, such as dashes and the copyright symbol. In the Symbols dialog box, click on the Special Characters tab to display a list of characters, then double-click on the character you want to insert.

oops! ▶ **Small boxes?**

If Word cannot display or print a symbol, it will display a small box.

▲ ▲ ▲ ▲ ▲ ▲

▶ ▶ ▶

▼ ▼ ▼ ▼ ▼

USING HIDDEN TEXT

Now you see it, now you don't. When you format text as *hidden*, you can choose whether or not it appears on screen and is printed with the document. Use hidden text to write reminders or notes that you want with the document but not printed with the final copy.

To format text as hidden:

▎ Click the Show/Hide button in the Toolbar to display the non-printing characters. If you do not show the characters, hidden text will not appear as you type it.

Options dialog box with hidden text display in the background

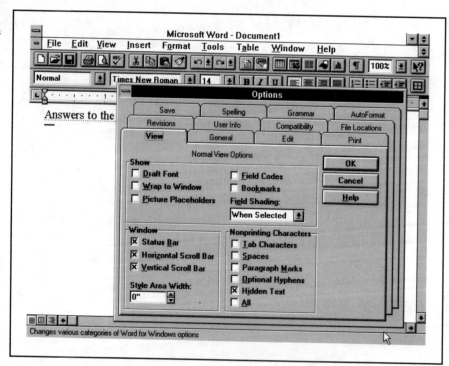

2 Press Ctrl+Shift+H, or select Format ➤ Font ➤ Hidden ➤ OK.

3 Type the text you want to hide. The characters will appear with a dotted underline.

4 To begin typing normal text, press Ctrl+Shift+H.

To hide or display hidden text, do one of the following:

▶ Click on the Show/Hide Toolbar button.

▶ To display hidden text without the non-printing characters, select Tools ➤ Options ➤ Hidden Text ➤ OK.

tip ▶ **Printing hidden text**
Hidden text will be printed if it is displayed when you print the document. Showing or hiding hidden text will affect the document's pagination. Before you print the document, make sure the hidden text is set as you want it to be for the print-out, then scan the document for proper pagination.

tip ▶ **Using hidden text**
If you are a teacher, you can type a test with the answers as hidden text. Turn off the display of hidden text to print the student copy of the text; turn on the display to print your copy.

COPYING STYLES WITH FORMAT PAINTER

Once you format text as you want it to appear, you can copy the format to apply it to other text. For example, if you select a character style, font, and point size for a heading, you can apply the same format to another heading without repeating all of the menu or Toolbar selections.

To copy a format:

| Place the insertion point in the text that contains the formats you want to copy.

Text about to be formatted with Format Painter

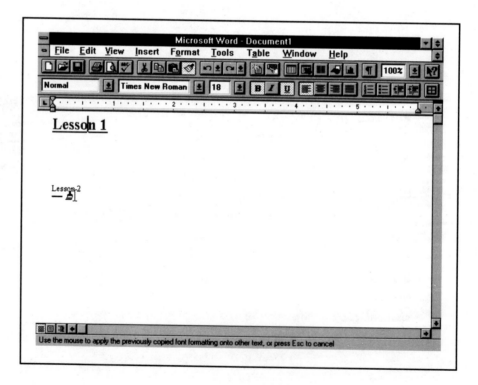

2 Click on the Format Painter Toolbar button. The mouse pointer changes to a small paintbrush and an I-beam.

3 Select the text you want to apply the format to—use the Scroll Bars to scroll the screen if necessary. When you release the mouse button, Word will apply the format.

tip ▶ **Making multiple copies**
To copy a format to more than one selection, double-click on the Format Painter Toolbar button. When you are done copying the formats to other text, press Esc or click on the Format Painter button again.

tip ▶ **Format painting with the keyboard**
To use the keyboard to copy formats, place the insertion point in the text containing the format you want to copy, and then press Ctrl+Shift+C. Select the text you want to format, then press Ctrl+Shift+V.

▲ ▲ ▲ ▲ ▲ ▲

Formatting Lines and Paragraphs

Attractive line formatting can make your document easy and more interesting to read. No matter how important your words, they have to be read to have any impact. By adjusting spacing and the alignment of text, you can help insure that your document has the maximum effect.

CHANGING LINE SPACING

Line spacing changes the overall appearance of the document. It can be set for the entire document, or just for sections within it. You can set line spacing for new text, or for text you've already typed.

To set the spacing of new text:

▶ Press Ctrl+1 for single spacing.

▶ Press Ctrl+5 for $1\frac{1}{2}$ line spacing.

Paragraph
Indents and
Spacing dialog
box

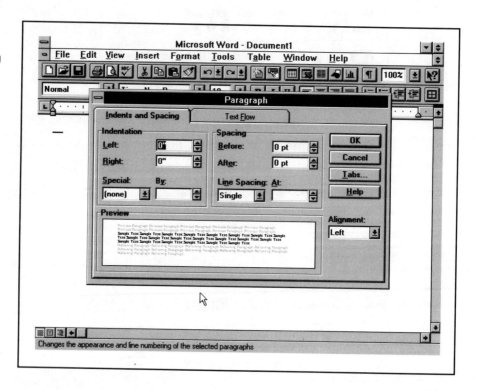

▶ Press Ctrl+2 for double spacing.

▶ Press Ctrl+0 to add an extra line between paragraphs.
(Press Ctrl+0 again to turn off this feature.)

To change the spacing of existing text:

▶ To change the spacing of a single paragraph, place the insertion anywhere in the paragraph before changing the spacing.

▶ To change spacing of several paragraphs, select the text first, then change the line spacing.

tip ▶ **Formats are paragraph oriented**

All of the formats discussed in this lesson are paragraph oriented. The formats of a paragraph are carried to the next one when you press Enter. To change the format of a new paragraph, you have to select other format options.

tip ▶ **Using the dialog box**

You can set other types of spacing by using the Paragraph Indents and Tabs dialog box. Select Format ➤ Paragraph, then select Indents and Spacing if the dialog box does not appear as in the figure. (You can also select Paragraph from the shortcut menu.)

▶ ▶ ▶

▼ ▼ ▼ ▼ ▼

CENTERING TEXT

Titles and subtitles often look best when centered between the left and right margins. They provide a break in the text and call attention to a change in subject or purpose.

To center a title or line of text:

1 Place the insertion point at the start of the line.

2 Press Ctrl+E. The insertion point moves to the center of the screen.

3 Type the text you want centered.

Alignment options in the Indents and Spacing dialog box

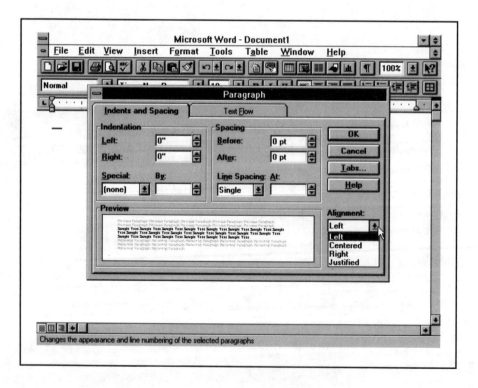

4 Press Enter.

5 Type any other text you want centered, or press Ctrl+L.

To center existing text:

 To center a single paragraph, place the insertion anywhere in the paragraph and press Ctrl+E.

To uncenter centered text, press Ctrl+L.

arning! ▶ **Using the Toolbar**

To center text with the **Toolbar**, click on the **Center** button. To stop centering, click on the **Align Left** button.

arning! ▶ **Uncentering text**

To uncenter text, place the insertion point in the paragraph (or select multiple centered paragraphs), click on the **Left** button or press **Ctrl+L.**

▲ ▲ ▲ ▲ ▲ ▲

ALIGNING
TEXT FLUSH RIGHT

Flush right text is aligned on the right margin with an uneven margin on the left—just the opposite of regular unjustified text. This format is most commonly used in business announcements and programs.

To align a line of text on the right:

| Press Ctrl+R. The insertion point will move to the right margin. You can also select Right alignment from the Paragraph Indents and Spacing dialog box.

Right-aligned text

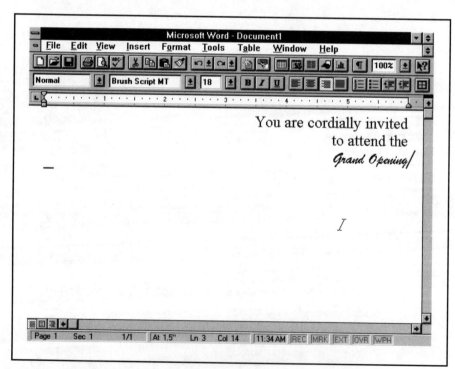

2 Type the text. Characters entered will move to the left.

3 Press Enter.

4 Press Ctrl+L.

To right align existing text:

▶ To right align a single paragraph, place the insertion anywhere in the paragraph and press Ctrl+R.

---

arning! ▶ **Flush right made simple**

To right align text on the right using the Toolbar, click on the **Align Right** button.

arning! ▶ **Changing your mind**

To return right-aligned text to normal, select the text and click on the **Left** button or press **Ctrl+L.**

▲ ▲ ▲ ▲ ▲ ▲

CREATING
FULL JUSTIFICATION

When you fully justify text, extra spaces are inserted between words to align your text along both margins at the same time. Word justifies every line of a paragraph except those that end in a hard carriage return—usually the last line.

To justify text:

| Place the insertion point where you want justification to begin.

Justified text

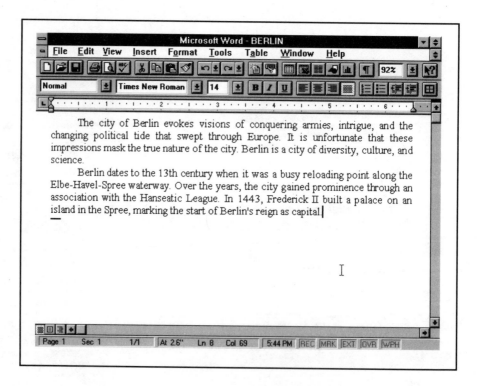

2 Press Ctrl+J. You can also select Justified alignment from the Paragraph Indents and Spacing dialog box.

3 Type the text, and press Enter.

4 Press Ctrl+L. The last line of a paragraph will not be justified.

To justify existing text:

▶ To justify a single paragraph, place the insertion anywhere in the paragraph and press Ctrl+J.

arning! ▷ **Justification with a click**

To justify text using the **Toolbar**, click on the **Align Justify** button.

arning! ▷ **Changing your mind**

To return justified text to normal, select the text and click on the **Left** button or press **Ctrl+L**.

tip ▷ **Full document justification**

To justify an entire document, select **Edit ➤ Select All** *before* selecting full justification.

▲ ▲ ▲ ▲ ▲ ▲

SETTING TABS
WITH THE RULER BAR

Using a mouse, you can set, delete, and change the position of tab stops using the Ruler. You can create four types of tab stops. With a default Left tab, characters shift to the right from the tab stop position. A Right tab aligns a column on the right by shifting characters to the left of the tab stop. Use a Center tab to center text around the tab stop. A Decimal tab aligns numbers on the decimal point—characters shift to the left as you type until you enter a decimal point.

Ruler Bar
showing tab
type indicators

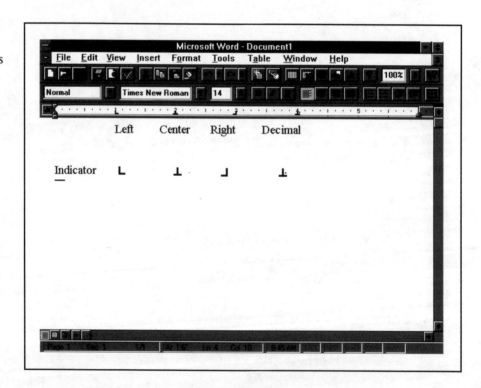

To set tabs with the Ruler:

1 Select View ➤ Ruler Bar to display the ruler. The default tab stops are set every $1/2$ inch.

2 Click on the box on the far left of the Ruler to select the tab type. The small graphic indicates the type, cycling from Left, Centered, Right, and Decimal.

3 Click at the position on the Ruler where you want to set the tab. The graphic indicator shows the tab type.

oops! ▶ **What happened to the default tabs?**
When you set a tab stop, the default tab stops to its left are deleted.

tip ▶ **Deleting and moving tabs**
To delete a tab, drag the tab indicator down into the document window then release the mouse button. To move a tab, drag its indicator to a new position on the Ruler.

▲ ▲ ▲ ▲ ▲ ▲

SETTING TABS WITH THE DIALOG BOX

While you can set tabs quickly with the Ruler, you have greater control over tabs using the Tab Set dialog box. Using the dialog box, you can quickly delete all of your custom tab stops, select a dot leader style, and set evenly spaced tabs. You can even create a Bar Tab to draw a line between columns.

To set tabs with the dialog box:

1 Select Format ➤ Tabs to display the Tabs dialog box.

2 To set a tab, type its position in the Tab Set Position box and select Set.

Tabs dialog box with Bar tab shown in the background

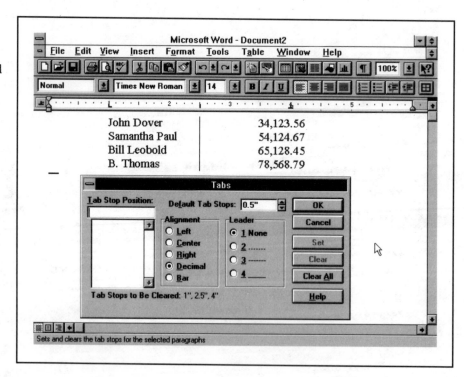

3 To customize a tab, select its position in the list box then choose a tab alignment and leader style.

4 To delete a tab, select its position in the list box and then click on Clear. Click on Clear All to delete all of your custom tabs, reinstating the default settings.

5 To set evenly spaced tabs, enter the spacing in the Default Tab Stops box.

for more... ▶ **Bar tab**

The Bar alignment option draws a vertical line on the screen at the tab stop position. In the Ruler, this tab type is indicated by a small vertical line. When you no longer want the line to appear, delete the tab stop.

tip ▶ **Leader types**

You can select to have no leader, or to create a dot leader, dashed leader, or solid line leader.

tip ▶ **Removing default tabs**

When you set a tab stop, the default tab stops to its left are deleted.

▲ ▲ ▲ ▲ ▲ ▲

It's So Easy

► Formatting Paragraphs

The default paragraph format used by Word is the block style. This means that every line—including the first one in a paragraph—starts at the left margin. In this lesson, you'll learn how to change the way paragraphs are arranged—by indenting them on the left or right, and by adding hyphens to even out lines on the right. You'll also learn how to automatically number paragraphs and highlight them with graphic symbols.

► ► ► ► ► ► ►

INDENTING PARAGRAPHS

To indent the first line of a paragraph, just press the Tab key. But you might want to indent a whole paragraph from the left margin, or from both the right and left margins as for a long quotation. You can indent a paragraph from the left using shortcut keys or the Toolbar.

To indent a paragraph from the left margin:

▶ Press Ctrl+M.

Each time you press Ctrl+M, the paragraph will indent to the next tab stop position on the right.

Using the ruler to indent paragraphs

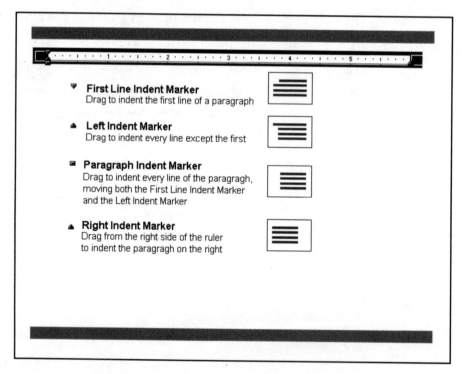

First Line Indent Marker
Drag to indent the first line of a paragraph

Left Indent Marker
Drag to indent every line except the first

Paragraph Indent Marker
Drag to indent every line of the paragragh, moving both the First Line Indent Marker and the Left Indent Marker

Right Indent Marker
Drag from the right side of the ruler to indent the paragragh on the right

To clear the indent:

▶ Press Ctrl+Shift+M until the insertion point is at the left margin.

You can also indent paragraphs on the left and the right using the ruler, as shown in the figure.

arning! ▷ **Click to indent**

Click on the Increase Indent button to indent a paragraph to the next tab stop. Click on the Decrease Indent button to reduce the indent the previous tab stop.

tip ▷ **Watch the ruler**

As you press Ctrl+M or click on the Increase Indent button, the indentation markers in the ruler will shift to the indented position.

tip ▷ **Using the dialog box**

You can also indent a paragraph using the Paragraph Indent and Spacing dialog box (select Format ➤ Paragraph).

▲ ▲ ▲ ▲ ▲ ▲

▼ ▼ ▼ ▼ ▼

CREATING HANGING INDENTATION

Standard paragraphs have only the first line indented with remaining text flush on the left. *Hanging indentations* are just the opposite—the first line starts to the left of the rest of the paragraph. Use hanging indentations when you want paragraphs to stand out from each other, as with numbered paragraphs and outlines.

To create a hanging indentation with the keyboard:

▶ Press Ctrl+T to indent all of the lines in a paragraph except the first.

▶ Press Ctrl+Shift+T to reduce the hanging indentation.

To create a hanging indentation with the ruler:

▶ Drag the Left Indent Marker to the right.

Hanging
indents

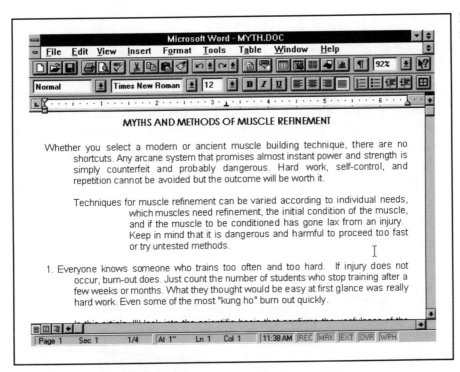

tip ▶ **Numbered paragraphs**

To create a numbered paragraph or outline, press **Ctrl+T** or drag the Left Indent marker to the right, type the paragraph number, then press **Tab**. Press **Ctrl+T** again to create further indentation levels. Press **Ctrl+Shift+T** to reduce the indentation level, or to reach the left margin.

tip ▶ **Watch the ruler**

When you press **Ctrl+T** or **Ctrl+Shift+T**, the Left Indent Marker in the ruler will shift positions.

CREATING BULLETED
AND NUMBERED LISTS

If you are writing a list or outline, you can have Word insert the paragraph numbers and create the hanging indentation for you in one step. You can choose the type of number to insert, or elect to mark paragraphs with small bullets (circles), arrows, diamonds, or asterisks.

To create a bulleted or numbered list:

❙ Select Format ➤ Bullets & Numbering to display the dialog box shown in the figure.

Bullets &
Numbering
dialog box with
Numbering and
Multilevel
options also
displayed

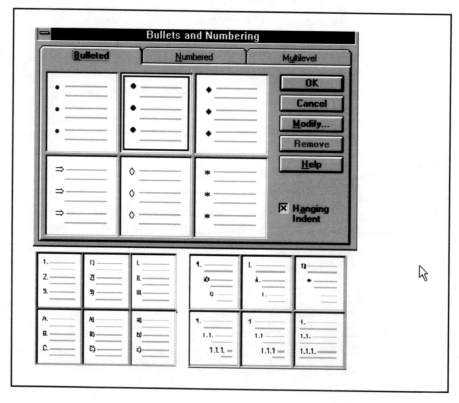

2 Select the Bulleted, Numbered or Multilevel tab to see additional options.

3 Click on the style you desire, then select OK. Word will insert the selected symbol, starting number or letter, and create a hanging indentation.

4 Type the text. Each time you press Enter, Word inserts the symbol or the next highest number.

5 To end the list, select Format ➤ Bullets & Numbering ➤ Remove.

To number or bullet existing text, select the text, then choose the bullet or numbering option.

arning! ▷ **The Numbering and Bullets buttons**

Press the Numbering button to begin a numbered list using the most recently selected number style. Press the Bullets button to begin a bulleted list. Click the button again to turn off numbering or bullets.

tip ▷ **Using the Shortcut menu**

You can also display the dialog box by selecting Bullets and Numbering from the Shortcut menu. Once you begin a list, the Shortcut menu contains additional options. Use *Promote* and *Demote* for multilevel lists. Select *Skip Numbering* to type a non-numbered paragraph. Select *Stop Numbering* to turn off bullets and numbering.

▲ ▲ ▲ ▲ ▲ ▲

HYPHENATING TEXT AUTOMATICALLY

A justified paragraph can have too many extra spaces between words. Hyphenating text reduces the extra spacing, and minimizes the ragged right margin of unjustified text. When you use automatic hyphenation, Word divides words for you and adds hyphens at the appropriate places.

To hyphenate a document automatically:

Ⅰ Select Tools ➤ Hyphenation to display the dialog box shown in the figure.

Hyphenation
dialog box

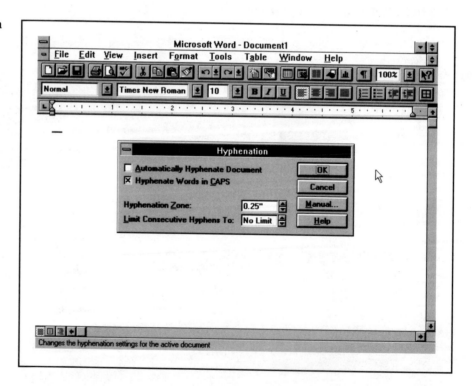

2 Click on Automatically Hyphenate Document, then select OK.

To manually select hyphenation positions:

1 Select Tools ➤ Hyphenation ➤ Manual. Word will change to Page Layout mode. At each word that needs hyphenating, Word will display a dialog box showing the suggested hyphenation point.

2 Select Yes to insert the hyphen at the suggested position, or click on another location in the word to insert the hyphen there.

---

tip ▶ **Hyphenation options**
Use the options in the Hyphenation dialog box to control the number of hyphens Word inserts. The setting in the Hyphenation Zone box determines how much space Word will leave at the end of a line in unjustified text. A larger setting results in fewer hyphens but a more ragged look. The Limit Consecutive Hyphens To box sets the number of consecutive lines that may be hyphenated.

tip ▶ **Hyphenating selected text**
To hyphenate a portion of a document, select the text before starting hyphenation.

It's
So
Easy

Formatting Pages

Each time you start Word, standard default settings are provided automatically to let you type and print documents without having to worry about the size of the page. The default margins result in a page with 54 lines of text, each line 6 inches wide. The text will appear neatly arranged when printed on standard business stationery, with text aligned on the left margin.

You don't have to change a thing if you like these settings and want to use them for every page of your document. But you can change any of these settings easily if you want other formats.

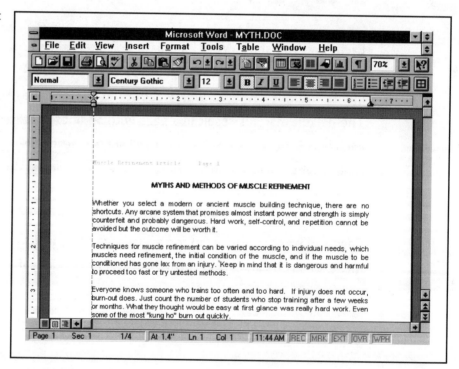

▼ ▼ ▼ ▼ ▼

SETTING THE MARGINS
WITH THE RULER

The page margins determine how much text will fit on each page. The right and left margins, for example, set the length of the printed line. To make a document appear longer, make the margins a little wider. Make them smaller to fit as much text as possible on a page.

To set the margins with the ruler:

❙ Select View ➤ Page Layout, or select File ➤ Print Preview.

Margins about to be changed in Page Layout view

2 Place the mouse pointer on the margin boundary on the ruler until the pointer is shaped like a two-headed arrow, then drag the mouse:

▶ Drag the left side of the horizontal ruler to change the left margin.

▶ Drag the right side of the horizontal ruler to change the right margin.

▶ Drag the top of the vertical ruler to change the top margins.

▶ Drag the bottom of the vertical ruler to change the bottom margins.

tip ▷ **Margins affect everything**
Changing the margins affects every page of the document unless you have inserted a section break.

tip ▷ **Display margin measurements**
As you drag the margin boundary, hold down the Alt key to display the exact measurements in inches.

tip ▷ **Margins versus Indent**
Use Indent to change the margins of an individual paragraph or selection of text. Use margins to change the margins of the entire document.

▲ ▲ ▲ ▲ ▲ ▲ ▲

CHANGING MARGINS WITH THE DIALOG BOX

If you do not have a mouse, or if you want to specify an exact margin position, you can change margins with the Page Layout dialog box.

To set the margins with the dialog box:

1 Select File ➤ Page Setup to display the Page Setup dialog box.

2 Select the Margins tab to display the options shown in the figure.

Page Setup Margins dialog box

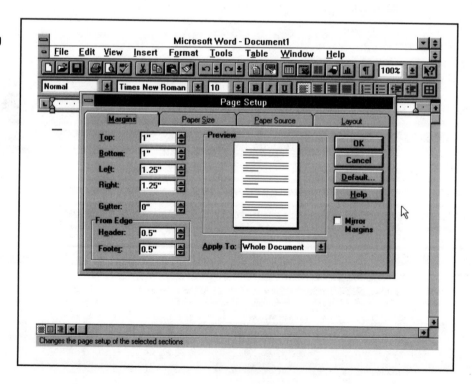

3 Set the left, right, top, and bottom margins as desired.

4 Select OK.

CREATING TITLE PAGES

Title pages usually contain several lines of text centered both horizontally and vertically on the page. Word lets you create title pages without changing the top and bottom margins.

To create a title page:

1 Select File ➤ Page Setup.

2 Select the Layout tab to display the dialog box shown in the figure.

3 Pull down the Vertical Alignment list and select Center.

Page Setup
Layout dialog
box

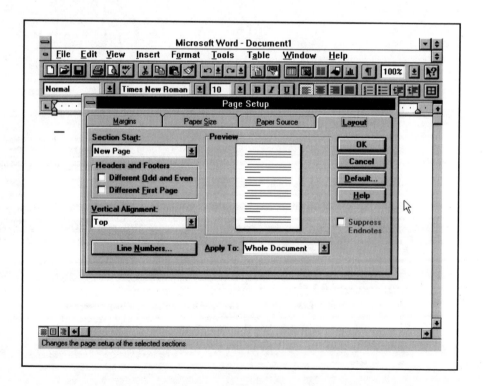

4 Pull down the Apply To list, and then select This Point Forward.

5 Select OK.

6 Type the text to be centered.

7 File ➤ Page Setup, pull down the Vertical Alignment list and select Top.

8 Pull down the Apply To list, and then select This Point Forward.

9 Select OK.

Word will insert a section break and start a new page. In normal view, a section break appears as a double dotted line with the words End of Section.

tip ▶ **Center every page**
To center every page of the document, select **Whole Document** in the **Apply To List**.

tip ▶ **Text on center**
To center text across the page, use **Ctrl+E**.

tip ▶ **Cancelling centered pages**
Pull down the **Undo** list in the toolbar and select **Page Setup**.

▲ ▲ ▲ ▲ ▲ ▲

SELECTING A PAGE SIZE

Because many paper and envelope sizes are standard, you can change from one paper size to another without having to measure and enter paper width and height yourself.

To change page sizes:

| Select File ➤ Page Setup, and click on the Paper Size tab.

Page Setup
Paper Size
dialog box

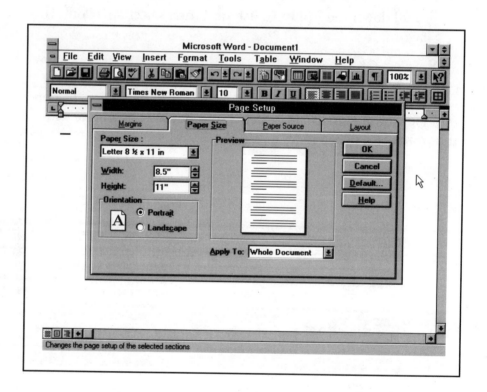

2　Pull down the Paper Size list and select a page size. To use a
　　size not listed, select Custom Size in the list, and then enter
　　the dimensions in the Width and Height boxes.

3　Select Portrait or Landscape orientation.

4　Select OK.

tip ▷　**Use sections**
　　　　Changing page sizes affects the entire document, or until
　　　　the next section break. To change the size of a specific
　　　　page, see "Working with Sections" later in this lesson.

tip ▷　**Changing the default page size**
　　　　To change the default page size or orientation for every
　　　　document using the normal template, select the page size
　　　　and orientation, click on the Default button, then choose
　　　　Yes from the dialog box that appears.

▲　▲　▲　▲　▲　▲

▼　▼　▼　▼　▼

PRINTING AN ENVELOPE WITH A LETTER

Word makes it easy for you to send letters. In just a few keystrokes, you can format and print an envelope using an address you've already typed on screen.

To print an envelope:

1 Type the letter, including the inside address.

2 If your letter contains more than one address, select the one you want to appear on the envelope.

Envelopes and Labels dialog box

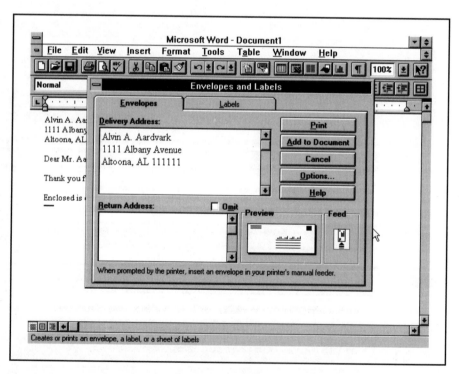

3 Select Tools ➤ Envelopes and Labels, then click on the Envelopes tab to display the dialog box shown in the figure.

4 Check the delivery address. If it is incorrect, select the Delivery Mailing Address box and edit the address.

5 To include your return address, select the Return Address box and type your address.

6 Select Add to Document to insert the envelope at the beginning of your document, separated from the text with a section break, or select Print to print the envelope immediately.

7 A dialog box will appear asking if you want to save the default return address—select No or Yes.

tip ▶ **POSTNET bar codes**

To insert a bar code, select Options in the Envelopes and Labels dialog box to display the Envelope Options box. Click on the Envelope Options tab, select Delivery Point Bar Code, then select OK to return to the Envelopes and Labels dialog box. Word will add the bar code above the delivery address.

tip ▶ **Other envelope options**

In the Envelope Options dialog box, you can select the envelope size, select a FIM-A Courtesy Reply Mail code, and change the font and position of the delivery and return addresses. If you click on the Printing Options tab, you can change the paper feed, and the direction of printing.

▲ ▲ ▲ ▲ ▲ ▲

▼   ▼   ▼   ▼   ▼

WORKING WITH SECTIONS

When you want to change the margins or page size of a single page, rather than of the entire document, you must insert a section break. The section break separates pages with different formats.

To format an individual page:

1 Place the insertion point at the start of the page you want to format and select File ➤ Page Layout.

2 Change the page size or margins.

Document
with two page
sizes and
orientations
using sections

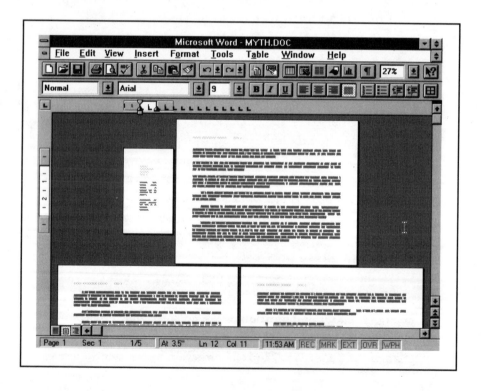

3 Pull down the Apply To list, and then select This Point Forward, then select OK. Word will insert a section break that also serves as a page break. The page size and margins will apply from the start of that page until the end of the document, or until the next section break.

4 Delete a hard page break if it appears immediately before the section break line.

5 If you do not want subsequent pages to have the same layout, place the insertion point at the start of the next page, then repeat this procedure to reset the page size and margins.

arning! ▶ **Changing your mind**

To return the text to its original layout, click on the Undo button in the Toolbar and select Page Layout. You can delete a section break by selecting it and pressing Del. However, this actually deletes the formats of the text *above* the break, so previous text will now be formatted using the settings of the text that was below the break.

▲ ▲ ▲ ▲ ▲ ▲

It's So Easy

Enhancing Your Pages

This lesson will show you how to add some finishing touches to your document to make it even more effective. You'll learn how to use headers, footers, and page numbers to identify the document. You will also learn how to automatically format your entire document, how to enclose text in boxes, add fill patterns, print in reverse, and insert horizontal and vertical lines.

CREATING
HEADERS AND FOOTERS

A *header* prints specified lines of text at the top of every page. *Footers* do the same—but at the bottom. Headers and footers will appear on the screen in Page Layout view, but not in normal view.

To insert a header or footer:

▌ Select View ➤ Header and Footer. Word will change into Page View. The Header and Footer Toolbar will appear, and the header and footer areas will be outlined.

Header and
Footer window

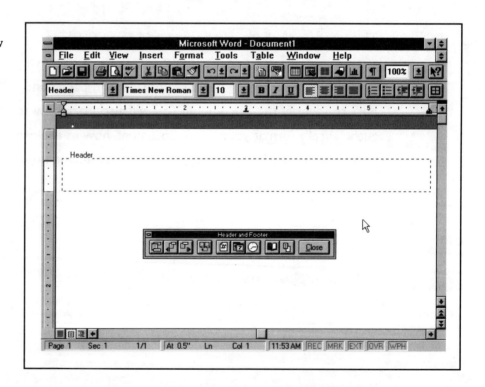

◀ ◀ ◀

2 Type the text of the header.

3 To enter a footer, click on the first button in the Toolbar, then type the text of the footer. Click on the same button to return to the header.

4 Select Close in the Header and Footer Toolbar.

tip ▶ **Header and Footer Toolbar**
The Header and Footer Toolbar contains the following buttons: *Switch* to the header or footer section; *Show Preview* to show the header/footer in the previous section; *Show Next* to show the header/footer in the next section; *Same as Previous* to set the header or footer the same as in the previous section; *Page #* to insert the page number; *Date* to insert the date; *Time* to insert the time; *Page Setup* to display the *Page Setup Layout* to set odd or even headers and footers, or to insert a different header and footer for the first page; *Show* to show or hide the document text.

tip ▶ **Deleting a header or footer**
Select View ➤ Header and Footer, then delete the text.

▲ ▲ ▲ ▲ ▲ ▲

▼ ▼ ▼ ▼ ▼

PAGE NUMBERS

A page number can be printed by itself on every page—without including it in a header or footer. Like headers and footers, the page number will not appear on the screen in normal view.

To number pages:

1 Select Insert ➤ Page Numbers to display the dialog box.

2 Pull down the Position list box and select a position, either Top of Page (Header) or Bottom of Page (Footer).

Page Numbers dialog box

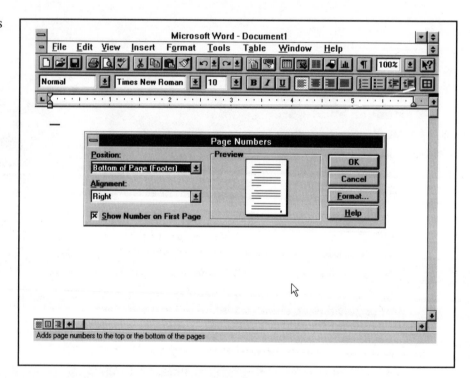

3 Pull down the Alignment list box and select a position: Left, Center, Right, Inside, or Outside. Inside and Outside alternate the placement on the odd and even pages.

4 To skip printing a number on the first page, click on Show Number on First Page.

5 Select OK.

oops! ▷

Headers versus page numbers

A page number set for the top of the page will print on the same line as a header. A number set for the bottom will print on the same line as a footer. Be careful if you set both.

tip ▷

Changing position

Page numbers, headers, and footers, print in the top and bottom margin areas of the page. To adjust the position, change to Page Layout view, then drag the header or footer margin boundary on the vertical ruler up or down.

▲ ▲ ▲ ▲ ▲ ▲

PAGE NUMBER FORMATS

You can number pages in letters or roman numerals. Lower case roman numerals, for example, are often used for front matter, such as a table of contents or introduction.

To format page numbers:

❙ Select Insert ➤ Page Numbers ➤ Format to display the dialog box shown in the figure.

Page Number Format dialog box

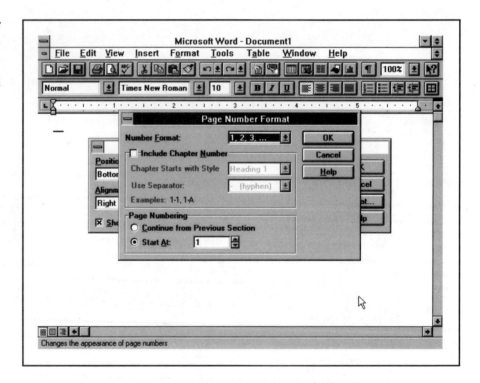

2 Pull down the Number Format list and select numbers (1,2,3…), lowercase letters (a,b,c…), uppercase letters (A,B,C…), lowercase roman (i,ii,iii…) or uppercase roman (I,II,III…).

3 Select OK.

4 Click on the AutoFormat button.

tip ▶ Numbering in sections

To use more than one number format on a document you must divide the document into sections. For example, suppose you have a 50 page document, followed by an appendix. If you do not use sections, the first page of the appendix will be numbered 51. To begin numbering the appendix with the lowercase roman i, place the insertion point at the start of the appendix and select Insert ➤ Break ➤ Continuous to enter a section break, then select Insert ➤ Page Numbers ➤ Format. Pull down the Number Format list and select (i,ii,iii…), then in the Start At box enter 1. To consecutively number pages through sections, select Continue From Previous.

tip ▶ Removing page numbers

To remove page numbers, pull down the Undo button in the Toolbar and select Page Numbers. You can also select and delete the number in the header or footer area.

▲ ▲ ▲ ▲ ▲ ▲

FORMATTING PAGES AUTOMATICALLY

You can format an entire document using Word's AutoFormat feature. AutoFormat scans your document, applying a built-in set of styles to titles, subtitles, and paragraphs. You can even select from a gallery of document styles.

To format a document automatically:

❙ Select Format ➤ Style Gallery to display the dialog box.

Style Gallery
dialog box

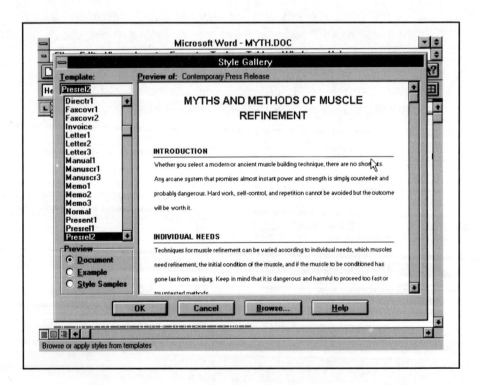

2 Click on a style to see how your document will appear in that format. You can also click on Sample to see a document that uses the full potential of the style.

3 Select OK to apply the formats to your document.

tip ► **AutoFormat dialog box**

To apply an automatic format and review the changes before accepting them, select Format ➤ AutoFormat, then select OK from the dialog box that appears.

power bar ► **Change your mind?**

To return the document to its previous format, click on the Undo button and select AutoFormat.

power bar ► **Quick AutoFormat**

Click on the AutoFormat button to apply styles contained in the current template.

▲ ▲ ▲ ▲ ▲ ▲

SURROUNDING TEXT IN A BOX

Make a section of text stand out by placing it in a box. Box an entire paragraph, or just a title or headline to draw the reader's attention.

To surround text in a box:

┃ Select View ➤ Toolbars ➤ Borders ➤ OK. The figure shows the Borders Toolbar with paragraphs illustrating some border and fill styles.

Borders
Toolbar with
same styles

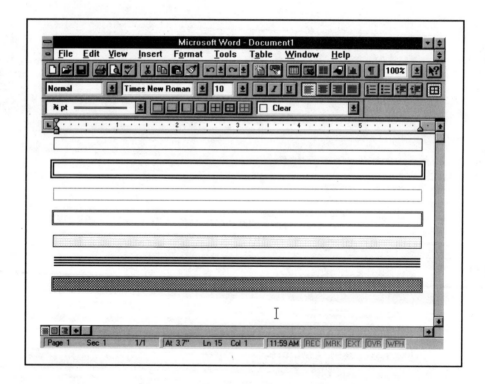

2 Select the text you wish to surround in a box. If you do not select text first, the box will surround the paragraph in which the insertion point is placed.

3 Pull down the Line Style list (the list on the left) and select a line thickness.

4 Click on the Outside Border button, the second button on the right of the Borders Toolbar.

5 Pull down the Shading list and select a shading style or pattern.

power bar ▶ **Border button**

Click on the Borders button to display the Toolbar.

power bar ▶ **Removing the box**

To remove the box, select the text and click on the No Border button.

tip ▶ **Box width**

Word extends the box from the right to left margin, even if you selected a one-word title centered on the page. To make a narrower box, indent the text.

▲ ▲ ▲ ▲ ▲ ▲ ▲

▼ ▼ ▼ ▼ ▼

ADDING VERTICAL AND HORIZONTAL LINES

Horizontal and vertical lines are great for separating text or adding some visual perspective. Use the Borders Toolbar or the Borders and Shading dialog box to lines above, below, or to the left or right of text.

To create a line:

▌ Display the Border Toolbar if it is not already on your screen.

Paragraph
Borders and
Shading dialog
box

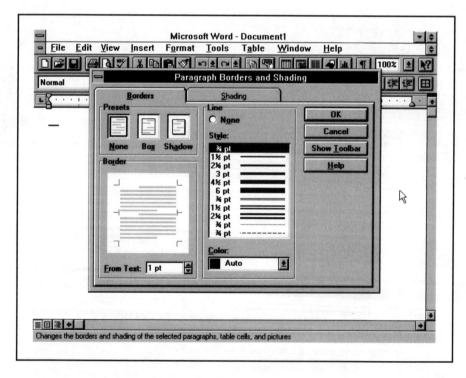

2 Place the insertion point in the paragraph or select the text you want to highlight with a line.

3 Click on the button in the borders Toolbar representing the position of the line. From left to right, the buttons represent the top, bottom, left side, right side, and inside of the text. Click on the inside border button to place lines between selected paragraphs.

tip ▶ **Using the dialog box**
Select Format ➤ Borders and Shading to display the dialog box. Select Box to surround the text in a box, click on Shadow to create a shadow box. To insert horizontal or vertical lines, click on location in the sample shown in the Borders box.

tip ▶ **Printing in color**
If you have a color printer, you can select the color of the lines, and foreground and background colors. If you print the document on a non-color printer, the colors will be converted to shades of gray, the darker the color, the darker the shade.

▲ ▲ ▲ ▲ ▲ ▲

Formatting can add impact to even the simplest document. By adjusting the appearance of characters, lines, paragraphs, and pages, you make your document easy and enjoyable to read.

Formatting Characters

Let's practice formatting now. We'll format some text as we type it, then select and format text.

1 Start Word for Windows.

2 Pull down the Font list in the Formatting Toolbar. With the keyboard, press Ctrl+Shift+F, then press the down arrow.

3 Select a TrueType font, such as Arial. TrueType fonts are indicated by the double T's before the font name.

4 Pull down the Font Size list in the Formatting Toolbar. With the keyboard, press Ctrl+Shift+P, then press the down arrow.

5 Select or type **14**.

6 Type **The** and press the spacebar.

7 Click on the underline button in the Toolbar, or press Ctrl+U.

8 Type **receptionist**, then click on the underline button or press Ctrl+U again.

9 Press the spacebar, then continue typing the remainder of the text:

> **The receptionist often presents the first impression that a visitor has of the business office. The receptionist must be professional, yet polite and cordial, even under pressure. If the visitor has an appointment, the receptionist must obtain the visitor's name and the staff person they have scheduled to meet.**
>
> **However, if the person does not have an appointment, the receptionist must learn the nature of the visit. The receptionist must then determine the proper person, if any, to refer the visitor to. There may be official guidelines explicitly indicating the course of action, or the receptionist may use judgment and experience in making this determination.**

Changing the Format of Characters

You can easily change the appearance of text you've already typed. Follow these steps.

1 Select the entire document. Either drag it with the mouse, or select Edit ➤ Select All.

2 Pull down the Font list.

3 Select another available TrueType font.

4 Pull down the Font Size list.

5 Select or type **12**, if it is available.

6 Click the mouse to deselect the text.

7 Place the insertion point at the start of the first line and press Enter twice.

8 Place the insertion point at the start of the first blank line, then pull down the Font Size list and select 18.

9 Click on the Bold button in the Toolbar, or press Ctrl+B.

10 Type **The Receptionist**.

11 Place the insertion point at the end of the document.

12 Press Enter twice.

13 Select Insert ➤ Symbol.

14 Pull down the Font list and select Wingdings.

15 Double-click on the symbol of the telephone, the ninth symbol in the top row.

16 Select Close.

17 Select the telephone symbol.

18 Pull down the Font Size list and select 24.

19 Click the mouse to deselect the symbol, then select File ➤ Print ➤ OK. Check your work against Figure 3.1.

20 Select File ➤ Save, type **Recept** and click on OK.

21 Select File ➤ Exit if you're not ready to go on.

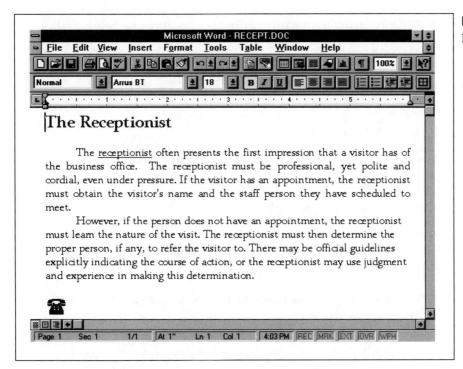

Figure 3.1:
RECEPT.DOC

Formatting Lines

Now let's change the line spacing, center the title, and justify the text. Here's how.

1 Open RECEPT.DOC if it is not already on your screen.

2 Select the entire document, then press Ctrl+2 to double space the text.

3 Deselect the text.

4 Place the insertion point at the start of the title.

5 Click on the Center button in the Toolbar, or press Ctrl+E.

6 Select the two paragraphs of text, then click on the Justify button in the Toolbar, or press Ctrl+J.

7 Deselect the text.

8 Select File ➤ Save.

9 Select File ➤ Exit if you're not ready to go on.

Formatting Paragraphs

Indenting paragraphs helps call attention to specific portions of text. It also breaks up long sections of text, making it easy to read and more pleasing to the eye.

Try formatting paragraphs now by creating two different indentation styles, starting with a hanging indentation.

1 Open RECEPT.DOC if it is not already on your screen.

2 Place the insertion point at the far left in front of the first paragraph, before the tab space.

3 Press Ctrl+T, or drag the left indent marker on the ruler to the $\frac{1}{2}$-inch position. The text shifts to the $\frac{1}{2}$-inch position.

4 Type **1.** to number the paragraph.

5 Place the insertion point at the left margin in front of the second paragraph, before the tab space.

6 Press Ctrl+M, or click on the Increase Indent button on the Toolbar.

7 Press Del to remove the tab space.

8 Select File ➤ Close ➤ No to clear the window without saving the document.

9 Select File ➤ Exit if you're not ready to go on.

Formatting Pages

Page formats affect the entire page. Set margins to change the amount of text that fits on the page, and change page sizes to print in different-sized paper or envelopes.

Let's widen the left and right margins, and print the document on legal-sized paper.

1 Open RECEPT.DOC if it is not already on your screen.

2 Select File ➤ Page Setup, then click on the Margins tab.

3 Select Left, then type **2**.

4 Select Right, then type **2**.

5 Click on the Paper Size tab.

6 Pull down the Paper Size list and select Legal 8.5 × 14 in.

7 Press Enter or click on OK.

Look at the document in Print Preview.

8 Select File ➤ Print Preview to look at the document. Your document should appear as shown in Figure 3.2.

9 Select Close to return to the document.

Figure 3.2:
Reformatted document showing wide margins and legal-sized paper

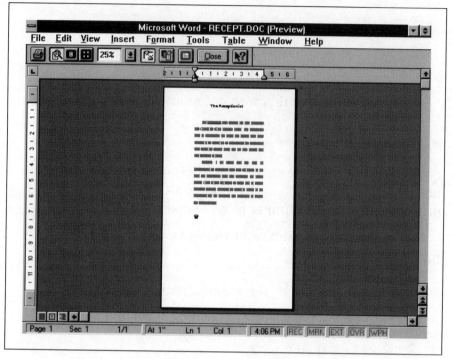

I0 Select File ➤ Close ➤ No to clear the window without saving the document.

II Select File ➤ Exit if you're not ready to go on.

Adding Headers, Footers, and Page Numbers

Headers, footers, and page numbers add some finishing touches to the document. But don't overdo it! Make them simple so they don't distract from the text.

Follow these steps to add a header and page number to
RECEPT.DOC. Start by deleting the date and line across the
page—these are just too much in addition to a header.

1 Open RECEPT.DOC if it is not already on your screen.

2 Select View ➤ Header and Footer.

3 Type your name.

4 Press Tab. Headers and footers are automatically set with a
center tab in the center of the page, and a right aligned tab
at the right margin.

5 Click on the Page Number button in the Header Toolbar.
(With the keyboard, select Insert ➤ Page Numbers ➤ Alignment ➤ Center ➤ OK.)

6 Press Tab.

7 Click on the Date button in the Header Toolbar. (With the
keyboard, select Insert ➤ Date and Time ➤ OK.)

8 Select Close in the Header Toolbar. Remember, you only see
headers in Page Layout and Print Preview modes.

9 Select File ➤ Print Preview. Check your work against Figure 3.3.

10 Select Close to return to the document.

11 Select File ➤ Save.

12 Select File ➤ Exit if you're not ready to go on.

Figure 3.3:
RECEPT.DOC
with a header
and page
number in Print
Preview

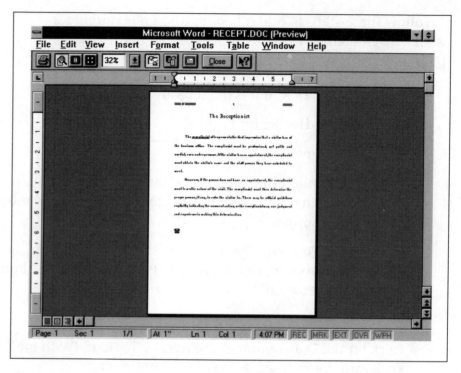

Adding Lines and Boxes

Graphic lines and borders add visual interest to your work. Practice using them now. Start by adding a horizontal line to the header in the Recept document, then adding a shading paragraph border.

1 Open RECEPT.DOC if it is not already on the screen.

2 Select View ➤ Toolbars ➤ Borders ➤ OK.

3 Select View ➤ Header and Footer.

4 Click on the Bottom Border button in the Borders Toolbar (the second button to the left of the Line Style pull-down list).

5 Select Close in the Header Toolbar.

6 Place the insertion point in the first paragraph.

7 Click on the Outside Borders button in the Borders Toolbar (the second button on the right) to insert a border around the paragraph.

8 Pull down the Shading list and select 10%.

9 Select File ➤ Print Preview to see how the page appears (Figure 3.4).

10 Select Close to return to the document.

11 Select File ➤ Save.

12 Select File ➤ Print ➤ OK.

13 Select File ➤ Exit.

Figure 3.4:
Document with
graphic line
and border

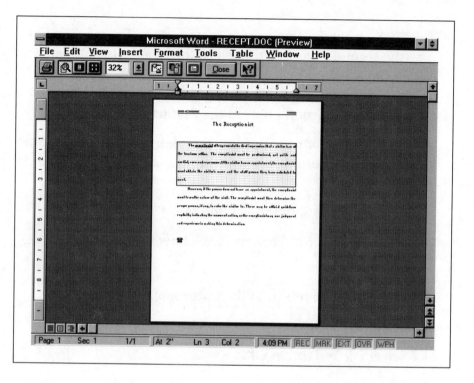

4 part four

SPECIAL WORD FOR WINDOWS FEATURES

If you think Word's editing and formatting capabilities are impressive, get ready to be amazed.

In these lessons, you will learn about Word's most powerful features. You'll learn how to harness the capabilities of Word to your computer and printer and to go beyond basic word processing. Enter the world of desktop publishing, form letters, and macros!

It's So Easy

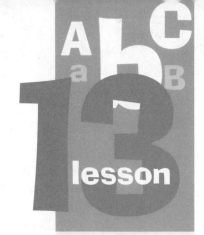

▶ Working with Tables and Columns

Word has several features for creating documents in columnar and tabular format. To create spreadsheets and other neatly ordered rows and columns of words or numbers, use Word's automatic table feature. Use the column feature to produce newsletters, resumes, and other documents. To create charts and graphs, use Word's powerful Picture command, explained in Lesson 16.

▶ ▶ ▶ ▶ ▶ ▶ ▶ ▶

▼　▼　▼　▼　▼

CREATING A TABLE

Before creating a table, plan the number of rows and columns that you'll need. You'll be able to insert and delete rows and columns—just like in a spreadsheet program—but you'll need a number to start with.

To create a table:

❚ Point to the Insert Table button on the Toolbar and hold down the left mouse button. A miniature grid appears.

Insert Table
Toolbar button

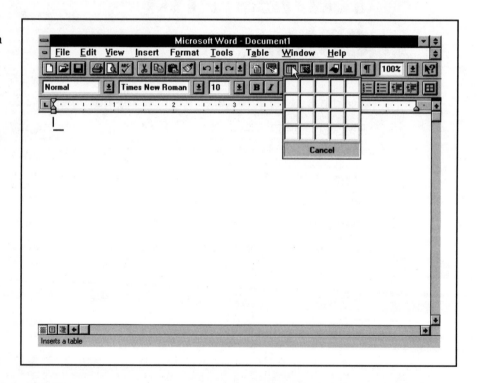

2 Drag the mouse down and to the right. As you drag the mouse, squares in the grid become selected and the number of rows and columns is indicated at the bottom of the grid.

3 Drag the mouse until you select the number of rows and columns you want in the table, then release the mouse button.

Word will display a blank table on the screen.

Each *cell* in the table is referenced by its row and column numbers. The top-left cell is A1. The ruler shows the width of the cells.

tip ▶ **Using the menu**

To create a table with the keyboard, select Table ➤ Insert Table, enter the number of columns and rows desired, then select OK.

tip ▶ **Table Wizard**

You can create a custom formatted table by using the Table Wizard. Select Table ➤ Insert Table, then select Wizard from the dialog box.

tip ▶ **Grid lines**

The dotted grid lines will not print. See "Formatting Tables" later in this lesson to learn how to create printable grid lines.

▲ ▲ ▲ ▲ ▲ ▲

▼　▼　▼　▼　▼

ENTERING DATA INTO TABLES

Once you create a table, you are ready to enter data into it. Many tables have *labels* along the top row and in the left-most column. The labels identify or explain the information in the other rows and columns. Don't worry how your entry aligns in a cell, or in rows and columns; you'll be able to format the table later.

Table with cell entries

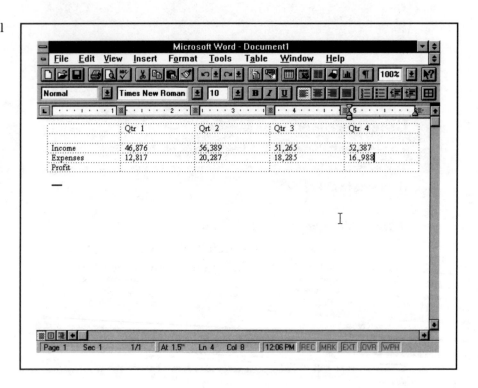

To enter data in cells:

1 Move to the cell you want to enter data into using any of these methods:

▶ Click on the cell with the mouse.

▶ Press ↑ and ↓ to move up and down columns.

▶ Press ←, →, Tab, and Shift+Tab to move across rows.

2 Type the data for the cell. The cell height will adjust automatically to the amount of text. *Do not press Enter to move to the next cell.* If you press Enter, the cell height will increase by one line. Press the Backspace key to delete the blank line.

tip ▶ **Wordwrap in narrow cells**
Word does not automatically adjust cell width to accommodate text. Widen a cell as explained in "Formatting Tables" later in this lesson.

tip ▶ **Editing cells**
To edit the data in a cell, move to the cell and then use Word's normal text editing techniques. To select cells, drag the pointer over the cells, or point to a cell line and click the mouse button.

▶ ▶ ▶

▼ ▼ ▼ ▼ ▼

FORMATTING TABLES

Once you create a table, you can change its size, format the text in cells, change column width, and add lines and fill patterns.
To change the size of a table:

> ▶ Select Table ➤ Insert Rows, or select Table ➤ Delete Cells to delete a cell, row, or column.

To change the width of columns:

> ▶ Place the mouse pointer in the line between columns so that the pointer is shaped like a two-headed arrow, then

Formatted
table with
border lines and
fill patterns

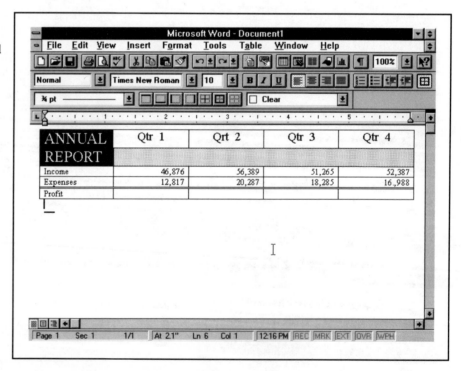

drag the mouse. You can also drag the column margin boundaries in the ruler.

To create printable grid lines:

▶ Display the Borders Toolbar, select the cells, then choose line options and fill patterns.

tip ▶ **Formatting cells**

Use the Toolbar, the Format menu, or their equivalent shortcut keys, to format text in cells. For example, to underline the text in a cell, select the text, then press Ctrl+B or click on the Bold button. To center text, press Ctrl+E.

tip ▶ **Formatting the entire table**

To format the entire table, select Table ➤ Table AutoFormat, then select a format from the dialog box that appears.

tip ▶ **Instant grid lines**

To place printable grid lines around the entire table, select the whole table, then click on the inside border and outside border buttons on the Borders Toolbar.

▲ ▲ ▲ ▲ ▲ ▲

PERFORMING MATH WITH FORMULAS

If you want to include totals, averages, or other mathematical results in a table, you can use *formulas* to compute the numbers for you. Formulas can make your table a full-fledged *spreadsheet*.

Suppose you have a table showing your income and expenses for the year. You can use formulas to total the income and expense categories, and other formulas to subtract the totals to obtain your net profit.

Formula
dialog box

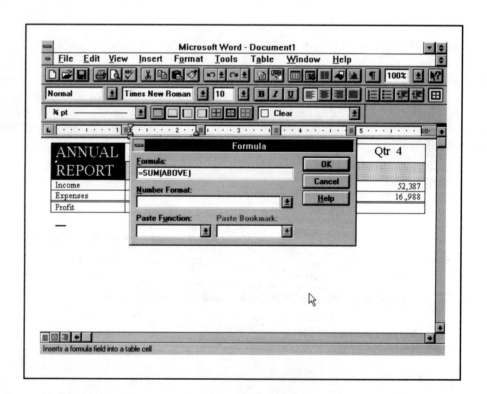

To enter a formula into a cell:

1 Place the insertion point in the cell in which you want to insert the formula.

2 Select Table ➤ Formula to display the dialog box shown in the figure. Word will display a default formula =SUM(Above) or =SUM(Left) depending on the content of surrounding cells.

3 In the Formula box, type the formula following the equal sign.

4 Select OK.

tip ▶ **Operators and cell references**

A formula can include mathematical operators, numeric values, and cell references. You reference a cell by its location in the table. For example, entering =B2-B3 in cell B4 will calculate and display the difference between cells B2 and B3 in cell B4.

tip ▶ **Recalculating formulas**

If you later change the value in a cell referenced in the formula, you must calculate the results again. Select the results in the cell, then press F9. To update every formula in the table, select Edit ➤ Select All, then press F9.

▼ ▼ ▼ ▼ ▼

CREATING NEWSPAPER COLUMNS

If you're responsible for producing a newsletter or other multico-lumn document, take advantage of Word's built-in column feature. Text automatically runs from one column to the next on the page, from left to right. When the far right column is filled, text moves to the left column on the next page.

Columns appear side-by-side in Page Layout view, but not in Normal view. To type columns:

| Before typing columns, type any desired single-column text, such as a title or introductory paragraph.

Columns
button

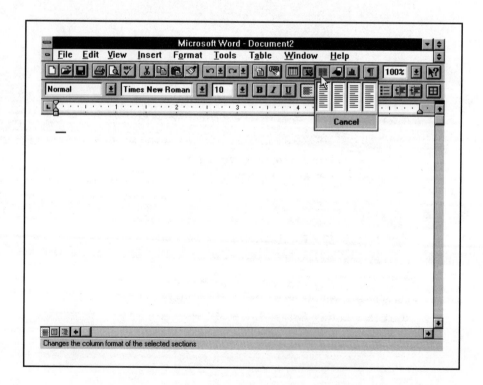

2 Select Insert ➤ Break ➤ Continuous ➤ OK to insert a section break without a page break.

3 Pull down the Columns button on the Toolbar. The figure shows the button options.

4 Select the number of columns desired.

5 Type the text of the columns.

6 To type single-column text again, select Insert ➤ Break ➤ Continuous ➤ OK, pull down the column button and select one column.

If you do not insert a section break, the entire document will be formatted in columns.

tip ▶ **To change column widths**
The ruler indicates the width of the columns and the spacing between them. To change the width of a column, point to the column margin boundary in the ruler and drag the mouse. To change the width of the columns and their position on the page, drag the page margin boundary.

tip ▶ **Ending a column**
To end a column before Word flows the text to the next column, press Ctrl+Shift+Enter.

▲ ▲ ▲ ▲ ▲ ▲

ENHANCING CUSTOM COLUMNS

The Toolbar Columns button creates columns of equal width. If you want to create uneven columns, or to place a line between columns, use the Columns dialog box.

To create custom columns:

1 Select Format ➤ Columns to display the dialog box shown in the figure.

2 Select Left or Right to create two uneven columns.

Columns dialog box

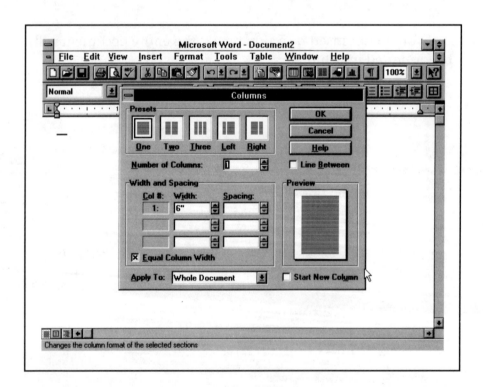

3 To create custom uneven columns, deselect the Equal Column Width box, enter the number of columns in the Number of Columns box, then set the column width and spacing in the text boxes.

4 In the Apply to box, select This Point Forward to insert a section break that does not also break pages.

tip ▶ **Inserting a line between columns**
In the Columns dialog box, click on Line Between. Word will insert a vertical line between the columns, as long as the longest column on the page.

tip ▶ **Borders shading**
Use the Border Toolbar, or the Paragraph Borders and Shading dialog box to insert lines around individual paragraphs, to surround text in boxes, or add shading and fill patterns. Borders extend from the left and right column border, not across the page.

▲ ▲ ▲ ▲ ▲ ▲

It's So Easy

Creating Form Letters

Form letters can save you from typing repetitive letters, even if you do not work in a business office. A well-designed form letter allows you to send the same information to many different people, but with a personal touch—so that the greeting reads *Dear Ms. Apple* or *Dear Mr. Jones* rather than the cold *Dear Sir or Madam. You can use form letters to respond to classified ads, request information, and write letters of complaint. Perhaps you are sending notes, thank-you letters, or invitations to family members or friends. Except for some personalized text, such as the name and address, each letter has the same words. So, save time and use a form letter!*

CREATING A DATA SOURCE FOR FORM DOCUMENTS

The first task in creating a form letter is to write the *data source*. Picture the data source as an electronic version of an index card file. Every card, called a *record*, contains all the data about one person or item. Each record has several pieces of information, such as the name, address, and other information about clients or employees. Each piece of information is called a *field*.

To create a data source:

| Select Tools ➤ Mail Merge to display the Mail Merge Helper.

Data Form
dialog box

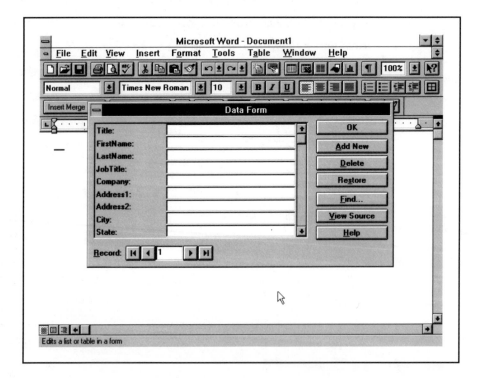

2 Pull down the Create list and select Form Letters.

3 Select Active Document or New Main Document.

4 Select Get Data ➤ Create Data Source. Word displays sample field names for common letters.

5 Select OK to accept the sample field names. Otherwise, select a field and click on Remove. Insert your own field names, pressing Enter after each, then select OK.

6 Enter the name of the data source file, then select OK.

7 Select Edit Data Source to see the dialog box shown in the figure.

8 Type the contents of each field, then press Enter. When you press Enter after the last field, Word will start a new record.

9 Select OK.

10 Enter the form letter now. But if you are not ready, select File ➤ Save All, select Yes to save the data source, then enter a name for the form letter and select OK.

11 Select File Close.

oops! ▶ **You must save the data source**
If you select File ➤ Save, to save the form letter, the data source file may not be saved as well. Select File ➤ Save As, or select File ➤ Close, then select Yes to save both files.

▲ ▲ ▲ ▲ ▲ ▲

WRITING THE FORM LETTER

Now that you have a data source, you can create the document that contains the form letter. The form letter will be associated—*linked*—with the data source file. When you come to a place where you want the variable information to appear, you have to enter a field code giving the name of the field that you want inserted at that location. Word will insert variable information during the merge process.

To write a form letter:

❚ Open the form letter, if it is not displayed on the screen. Word automatically displays the Mail Merge Toolbar.

Completed form document showing Merge Feature Bar

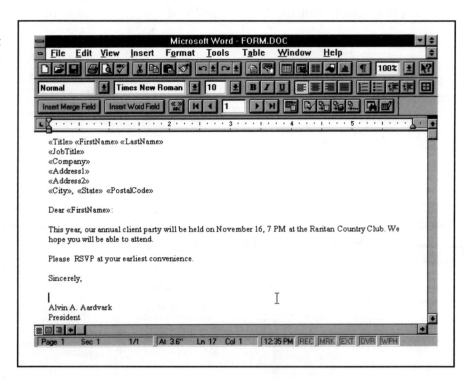

(See "Merging and Printing Form Documents" for a description of the Toolbar.)

2 Type the letter.

3 When you reach a location where you want to enter a field, select Insert Merge Field from the Toolbar, then click on the field name in the list that appears.

4 Save the completed form document.

oops! ▶ **Save that data source file**

If you are creating the form letter immediately after creating the data source file, selecting File ➤ Save will save the form file only. To save the data file, select File ➤ Save As, or select File ➤ Close and select Yes in the dialog boxes that appear.

tip ▶ **Using an existing data source**

To create a form letter using an existing data source file, select Tools ➤ Mail Merge ➤ Create ➤ Form Letters ➤ New Document Window. Then, select Get Data ➤ Open Data Source, select the name of the data source file, then click on OK twice. Select Edit Main Document, then write the form letter.

▲ ▲ ▲ ▲ ▲ ▲

MERGING AND PRINTING FORM DOCUMENTS

When you perform a merge, the variable information from a record is inserted in the appropriate place in a form letter. A page break is inserted and another letter is created, until all of the records have been used.

Newly merged documents can be printed immediately, saved on disk, or edited.

To merge form letters:

❘ Open the form letter.

Merge dialog box

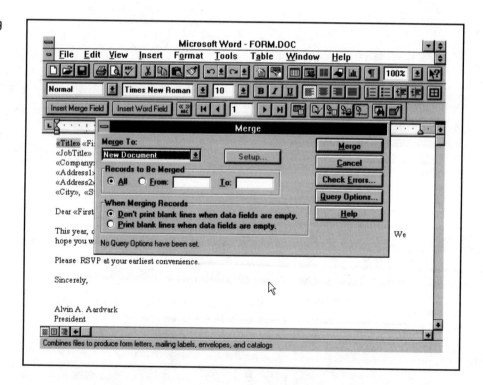

2 Click on one of the following:

► Click on the Merge To New Document button to merge the files and display them in a new document window.

► Click on the Merge to Printer button to merge and print the documents.

► Click on the Mail Merge button to display a dialog box for selecting a range of records to print.

By default, Word will not print a blank line if the field printed on the line contains no data.

tip ► **Mail Merge Toolbar**

The mail merge Toolbar contains these buttons (from left to right): *Insert Merge Field* displays a list of fields; *Insert Word Fields* displays a list of merge commands; *View Merge Data* replaces field codes with data; *First Record; Previous Record; Next Record; Last Record; Mail Merge Helper* displays the Helper dialog box; *Check for Errors* looks for potential merge code errors; *Merge to New Document; Merge to Printer; Mail Merge* displays the Mail Merge dialog box; *Find Record* locates a record; *Edit Data Source* displays the Data Form dialog box.

▲ ▲ ▲ ▲ ▲ ▲

▼ ▼ ▼ ▼ ▼

PRINTING ENVELOPES FOR FORM LETTERS

If you are printing form letters, you can also use merge codes to print envelopes. The envelopes will print in the same order as your letters, so all you have to do is match them up, insert the letter, and mail.

To print envelopes for form letters:

1 Select Tools ➤ Mail Merge ➤ Create ➤ Envelopes ➤ New Document Window.

2 Select Get Data ➤ Open Data Source, select the data source file, then click on OK.

Envelope
merge codes

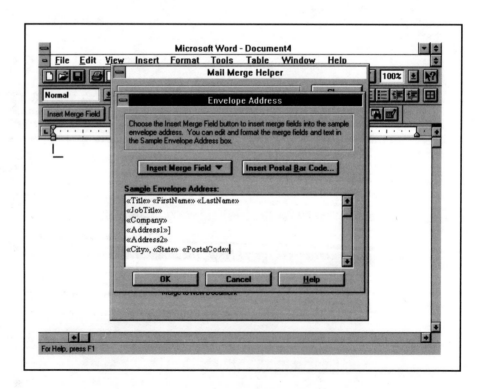

3 Choose Setup Main Document to display the Envelope options dialog box, then select OK.

4 Use the Insert Merge Field button to insert the merge codes for the address. The dialog box should appear as in the figure.

5 Click on Insert Postal Codes, pull down the Merge Field with ZIP Code text box, and select the name of the field containing the zip code.

6 Pull down the Merge Field with Street Address box and select the field with the address.

7 Select OK twice.

8 Select Merge twice, then close the Mail Merge dialog box.

tip ► **Merging to labels**

You can use almost the same steps as described for merging envelopes to create mailing labels. Select Tools ➤ Mail Merge ➤ Create ➤ Mailing Labels, instead of Envelopes then continue following the procedure. When the Label Options dialog box appears, select a label format from the list box, then select OK. Complete the procedure as described.

▲ ▲ ▲ ▲ ▲ ▲

It's So Easy

► Word Tools

Word provides a number of tools that go far beyond basic word processing functions. No matter what the task, these tools makes your work easier and faster. You can create macros to speed typing and menu selections, use styles to streamline formatting, check your spelling, or use the thesaurus and grammar checker to improve your vocabulary and writing style.

►►►►►►►►►

▼ ▼ ▼ ▼ ▼

RECORDING AND PLAYING MACROS

A *macro* is a special command you create to automate repetitive tasks. If there is a particular task that you do over and over in Word, such as entering your letterhead, or a standard line of text, you can create a macro that records the keystrokes. You can then replay the macro anytime in the future by simply typing its name. Macros can be used to repeat text, formatting commands, or any menu or dialog box selections.

To record a macro:

| Select Tools ➤ Macro ➤ Record to display the dialog box as shown in the figure.

Record Macro
dialog box

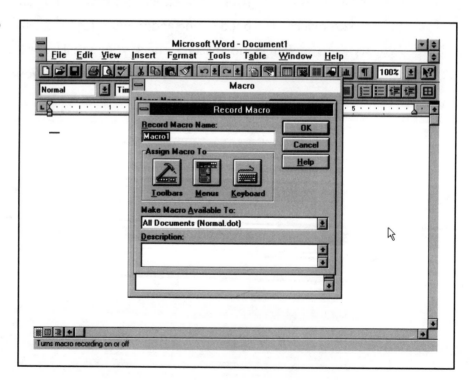

2 Type the macro name, then click on OK. A small macro Tool-bar appears with two buttons: Stop and Pause.

3 Type your keystrokes, or select menu and dialog box options. While recording a macro you cannot use the mouse to select text or move the insertion point.

4 Select Tools ➤ Macro ➤ Stop Recording, or click on the left button in the macro Toolbar.

To play a macro:

➤ Select Tools ➤ Macro, select the macro from the list that appears, then select Run.

tip ▶ **Record macro options**
The Record Macro dialog box contains these options: *Record Macro Name*—the macro name can be up to 36 characters, but cannot contain spaces, commas, or periods; *Assign Macro To*—lets you add a macro to a Toolbar, menu, or to a shortcut key combination; *Description*—the description, up to 255 characters long, will appear in the Macro dialog box when you select the macro to be run.

tip ▶ **Organizing macros**
Click on Organizer in the Macro dialog box to display options for renaming macros, and moving them between templates.

▲ ▲ ▲ ▲ ▲ ▲

▼   ▼   ▼   ▼   ▼

CREATING A STYLE

If you find yourself applying the same formats time and again, you'll love styles. For example, do you format headlines a certain way, or change the font and spacing of paragraphs on a regular basis? By saving a common format in a style, you can reapply the format by simply selecting a style name. Use styles to format text consistently, so similar documents have the same overall appearance.

To create a style:

| Place the insertion point in the text that contains the formats you want to save in a style.

Style list box on the Formatting Toolbar

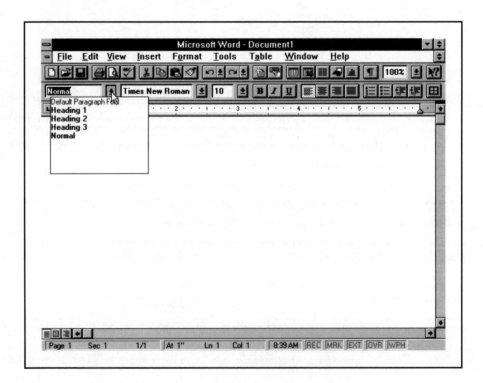

◀ ◀ ◀

2 Click on the Style list box in the Toolbar.

3 Type the name you want to give the style. A style name can be up to 253 characters long.

4 Press Enter.

To apply a style:

▶ Pull down the style list box and select the name of the style you want to apply.

tip ▶ **Changing the default style**

The default style applied to paragraphs is called Normal. To change the normal style, format a paragraph that already uses the Normal style, then select Normal in the style list. The Reapply Style dialog box will appear. Select Redefine the style using the selection as an example. To reformat the text using the default style, select Return the formatting of the selection to the style.

tip ▶ **Styles and attributes**

If the paragraph contains several character attributes, the attribute at the location of the insertion point will be applied to the style, and to the entire paragraph.

▲ ▲ ▲ ▲ ▲ ▲

▼ ▼ ▼ ▼ ▼

CORRECTING
SPELLING ERRORS

Even if you win at spelling bees, typographical and spelling errors can still find their way into your documents. Save yourself some embarrassing moments by checking spelling before printing and distributing your document.

To check a document for spelling:

| Position the insertion point in the text you want to spell check. If you do not want to check the entire document, select the text you want to check first.

Spelling dialog box

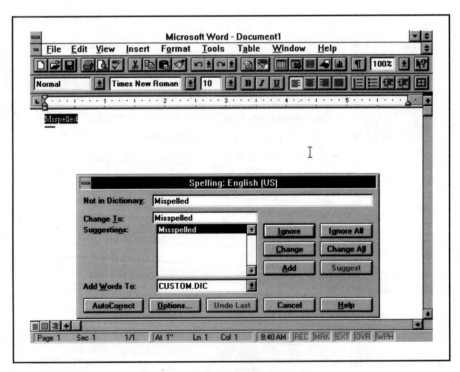

2 Select Tools ➤ Spelling (F7). Word finds the first possible error and displays a list of alternative spellings. Word scrolls the document so the misspelled word appears selected above the dialog box. The misspelled word also appears, however, at the Not in Dictionary prompt at the top of the dialog box.

3 Double-click on the correctly spelled word in the list to replace the misspelled word, or select Ignore All to accept the word as it is spelled for the remainder of the session.

tip ▶ **How much do you want to check?**

The spell check begins at the location of the insertion point. When Word reaches the end of the document, it begins checking at the beginning, and continues until it reaches the original position of the insertion point. To spell check a single word, select the word.

tip ▶ **Other spelling options**

To edit the word manually, type the correct spelling in the Change To box, then press Enter or click on Change. Select *Ignore* to leave the word as it is this one time; *Delete* (which replaced the Change button when the Change to box is empty) to delete the word in the document; *Change All* to change all occurrences of the word in the document to the word in the Change To box for all instances in the document; *Delete All* to delete every occurrence of the word; *AutoCorrect* to add the word and the replacement spelling to the AutoCorrect list; *Undo Last* to reverse the last actions performed in the spell check session.

▲ ▲ ▲ ▲ ▲ ▲

► ► ► ►

▼ ▼ ▼ ▼ ▼

IMPROVING YOUR VOCABULARY

Sometimes the hardest part of writing is selecting the right word. This calls for the Word thesaurus.

To find a synonym:

1 Place the insertion point anywhere in the word you want to replace with a synonym.

2 Select Tools ➤ Thesaurus (Shift+F7) to display the Thesaurus dialog box. Several synonyms for the word may be listed.

Thesaurus
dialog box

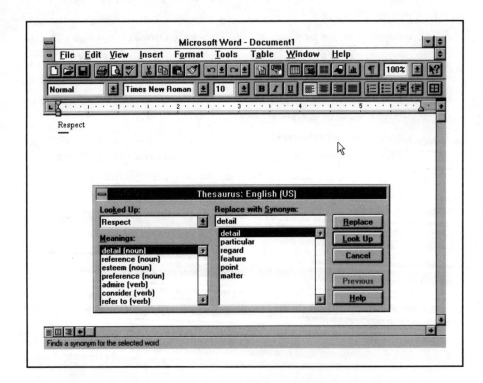

3 In the Meanings list box, click on the word or phrase that has the meaning you want to get across. The words listed in the Synonyms box will change as you select meanings.

4 In the Synonyms list box, select the word you want to insert in your document.

5 Select Replace.

tip ► **More words**
Sometimes the meaning box will list the options Related Words and Antonyms. Selecting Related Words usually shows the root of the word, such as form for the word former. Selecting Antonyms list words with the opposite meaning.

tip ► **Word Not Found**
If Word cannot find a synonym, an alphabetical listing of words and phrases will appear in the Meanings box. Select a word or phrase that has the same meaning as the synonym you're hoping to find.

▲ ▲ ▲ ▲ ▲ ▲

▶ ▶ ▶ ▶

▼　▼　▼　▼　▼

IMPROVING YOUR GRAMMAR

Word's speller cannot determine if you used the wrong word when it is correctly spelled. For instance, it won't report that you used *too* instead of *to* or *two*, or used *effect* when you should have used *affect*. Fortunately, Word can check your grammar.

1 Type or open the document you want checked.

2 Select Select Tools ➤ Grammar.

3 Word finds the first possible error and displays a description of the problem and, in some cases, a suggested correction.

The Grammar dialog box

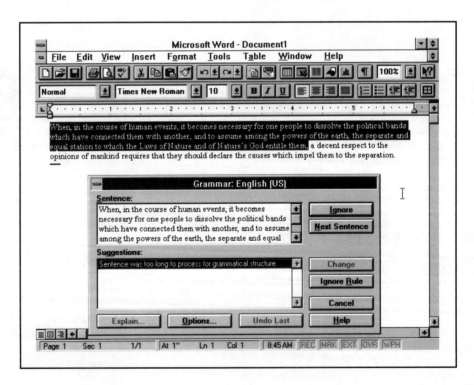

If Word encounters a spelling error, it will display the Spelling dialog box.

4 Select Change to replace the text with Word's suggestion, or select Ignore to move on to the next problem. The Change button will be dimmed if Word cannot make the correction for you.

When the process is complete, a dialog box appears reporting readability statistics, including the grade level; the number of words, characters, paragraphs, and sentences; and the average sentences per paragraph, words per sentence, and characters per word.

tip ▷ **Other options**

Sometimes the description of the problem is not enough to help you make the correction. For a more complete explanation, click on the Explain button. A Grammar Explanation appears with a description of the grammatical rule. Read the explanation, then double-click on the box's close button to continue.

tip ▷ **Grammar styles**

Casual, legal, technical, and some other writing styles may include certain conventions that violate strict grammatical rulers. You can select an overall set of rules to use for the grammar check process by selecting Options in the Grammar Options dialog box. You can then select a writing style to determine which rules of grammar are applied. You can also select to turn off the spelling check during the grammar process, and to prevent the display of readability statistics.

It's So Easy

Desktop Publishing with Graphics

As you become familiar with Word's graphics commands, you'll see that you can create some rather sophisticated documents. Not only can you produce some very dramatic effects, but you can have a lot of fun doing it.

There's really much more to graphics than can be covered in a book of this length. But this lesson will show you the basics you'll need to use graphic images in your documents.

RETRIEVING A GRAPHIC IMAGE

The first step in using a graphic image is to retrieve it into your document. You must know the name of the graphics file, including its file extension, and the drive and directory in which the file is located.

To retrieve a graphic image:

I Select Insert ➤ Picture to display the Insert Picture dialog box.

Graphic image inserted into document

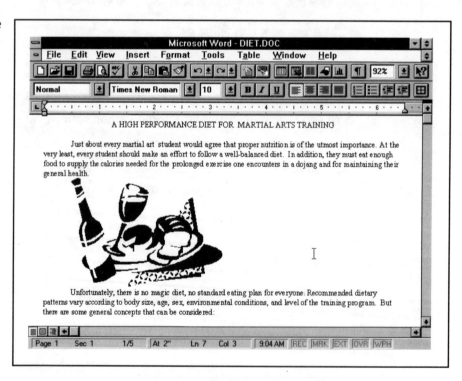

2 Double-click on the filename in the list box, or select the
name, then click on OK. The graphic appears at the position
of the insertion point.

oops! ▶ **Finding files**

The Insert Picture dialog box lists graphics files in the
\CLIPART sub-directory. By default, it will list every file
having any of the common graphic extension: bmp, eps,
pcx, pct, tif, wmf, and wpg. Use the Directories and Drive
boxes to display a list of graphic images in other locations.
Use the List Files of Type box to limit the display to specific file type.

tip ▶ **Previewing graphics**

If you want to preview the graphic before inserting it in
your document, select its name in the Insert Picture dialog
box, then click on the Preview Picture checkbox.

tip ▶ **Saving disk space**

When you insert a picture, the graphics file is stored with
your Word document. Documents that contain pictures
can take up a great deal of disk space. If your disk space is
limited, select Link To File, then deselect the Save Picture
in Document option. Only a link to the picture file will be
saved with the document.

▲ ▲ ▲ ▲ ▲ ▲

▼ ▼ ▼ ▼ ▼

CHANGING THE SIZE OF A PICTURE

In your document, the picture is contained in an invisible box. When you scale the picture, you change the size and shape of the box to either enlarge or reduce the picture. When you crop the box, you change the size of the box, but not of the picture. Crop a picture to change the amount of white space around the picture, or reduce the amount of the picture displayed and printed.

To change the size and shape of a picture:

| Click on the picture. It will be surrounded by a box with eight smaller boxes, called handles.

Pictures in several sizes, some cropped

2 To change the size of the picture, drag one of the handles.

   ▶ Drag a corner handle to change the height and width of the box but to maintain the same width to height ratio.

   ▶ Drag a handle on the side to change just the width.

   ▶ Drag a handle on the top or bottom to change just the height of the box.

3 To crop the picture, hold down the Shift key and drag one of the handles.

Pictures look best when in the same proportion as the original. To deselect a picture, click outside of the box.

---

tip ▶ **To delete a picture**
Select the picture, then press Del.

tip ▶ **Beyond the screen**
You cannot drag a handle past the edge of the window. To make the picture as large as possible, select Page Layout view and zoom to the see the whole page.

tip ▶ **Watch the status line**
As you scale a picture, the status line will display the percentage of the original. As you crop a picture, the status line reports the amount of space added or deleted.

▲ ▲ ▲ ▲ ▲ ▲

TO CHANGE THE POSITION OF A PICTURE

To adjust the position of a picture, you must insert it in a frame. A frame is a non-printable border that allows the picture to be positioned independently of the text on the page. Until you surround a picture in a frame, the picture is treated as a separate paragraph. Once you add a frame, Word will wrap text around the picture.

To insert a frame:

▌ Select the picture.

Picture in a frame

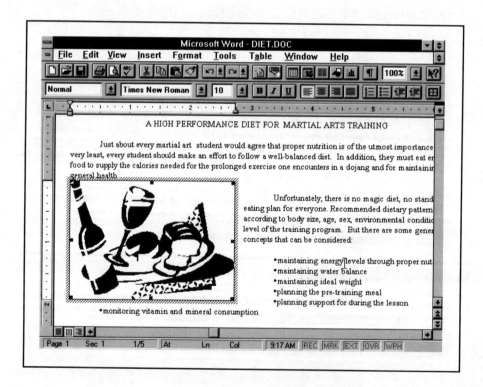

2 Select Insert ➤ Frame. If you are in Normal view, a dialog box will appear asking if you want to change to Page Layout view. Select Yes—you can only work with frames in Page Layout view. The frame appears around a selected picture as a thick box with diagonal lines.

To move a picture:

1 In Page Layout view, point to the picture. The pointer will change to four-pointed arrow.

2 Drag the picture to the desired location, then release the mouse button.

3 Click away from the picture to deselect it.

tip ▶ **Colliding pictures**

Once you add a frame, text will flow around the picture. You can also move two or more framed pictures so they overlap. Pictures are not transparent. Overlapping one picture on another will partially obscure one of them. However, extra white space added by cropping is treated as transparent.

▲ ▲ ▲ ▲ ▲ ▲

ADDING A BORDER TO A PICTURE

The border that appears when you select a picture will not print around it. A border, however, can create a dramatic and eye-catching effect. You can add a border using either the Border Toolbar or the Paragraph Borders and Shading dialog box.

To surround a picture with a border:

1 Select the picture.

2 Select Format ➤ Borders and Shading.

3 Click on the Borders tab.

Pictures
showing border
styles

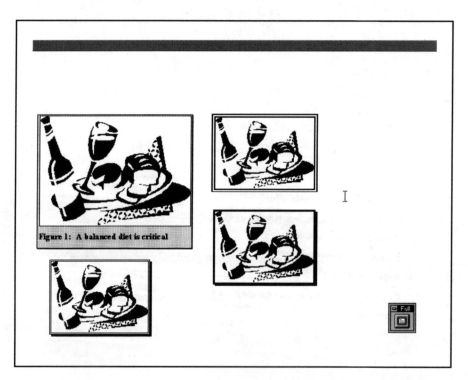

Figure 1: A balanced diet is critical

4 Select either Box or Shadow.

5 Select a line style.

6 Select OK.

The border will be the same size as the selection box around the picture. Because pictures are not transparent, you cannot add a shade or fill pattern inside the box.

tip ▶ **Adding a caption**

You can automatically number and caption pictures as figures. Add a frame to the picture, select the picture, then select Insert ➤ Caption ➤ OK. The word *figure*, followed by the figure number, will appear beneath the picture and inside the frame. If you select a fill shade or pattern, the fill will appear in the background of the caption, as shown in the figure.

▲ ▲ ▲ ▲ ▲ ▲

CREATING TEXT BOXES

You can add a frame to text as well as graphics. Once you insert a frame around text, you can move the text anywhere in the document by dragging it with the mouse. The size of the frame will change automatically as you add or delete text within it. Changing the frame size does not change the size of the characters within it.

1 Select the text you want to box.

2 Select Insert ➤ Frame.

3 Deselect the frame. Word automatically surrounds the text in a single-line border.

Text boxes

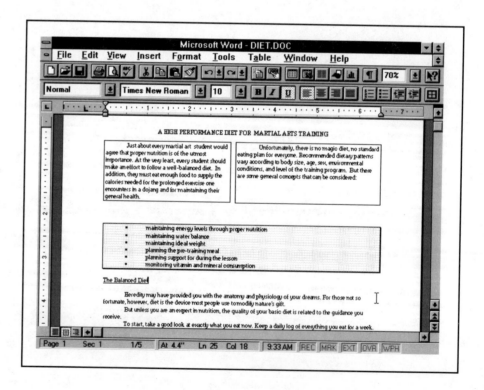

To customize the frame, do any—or all—of the following:

► Drag the frame to position the text on the page.

► Drag a handle to change the size of the frame.

► Select the frame, then use the Border Toolbar or dialog box to change the border, or to add a fill shade or pattern.

tip ► **Changing box size**
You cannot crop a text box to change the amount of text displayed. You can enlarge the box to add extra space around the text, but you cannot make it smaller than text itself. Changing the shape of the box will adjust the position of line breaks.

tip ► **Editing boxed text**
To edit text in the box, click inside the box. You can edit and format the text using all of Word's formatting options.

tip ► **Deleting frames**
If you delete the frame by pressing Del, the text within the frame is also deleted. To remove the frame, select the frame, then select Format ➤ Frame ➤ Remove Frame.

▲ ▲ ▲ ▲ ▲ ▲

▶ ▶ ▶

▼ ▼ ▼ ▼ ▼

DRAWING IN WORD

Word lets you create your own artwork and customize pictures that you insert in your document. To use these capabilities to their fullest potential requires some knowledge of computer graphics and a degree of creativity and artistic ability. Here's how to get started.

To create artwork:

1 Change to Page Layout View. You can only draw in Page Layout view.

2 Select View ➤ Toolbars ➤ Drawing ➤ OK.

The Drawing Toolbar and some effects that can be created

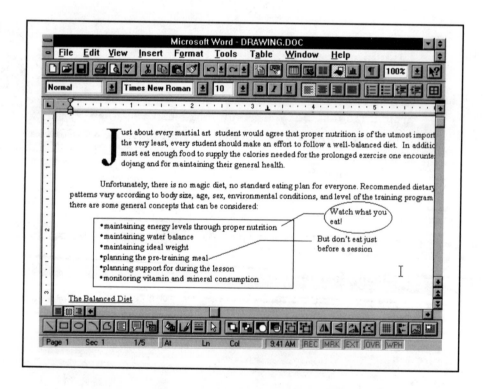

3 Use the tools in the drawing toolbar to draw images directly in the document.

Each item you draw is treated as a separate object. You can select each individually to change its size, shape, and position. As long as you do not frame the objects, they can overlap without obscuring other objects, text, and pictures.

power bar ▶ **Instant art**

Click on the Drawing button in the Standard Toolbar to display the Drawing Toolbar and change to Page Layout view. Click on the button again to remove the Toolbar.

tip ▶ **Picture perfect**

To draw straight lines, perfect squares and circles, hold down the Shift key while you use the Line, Rectangle, or Ellipse tools. To draw a circle using the position of the mouse as the center point, select the Ellipse tool, hold down Ctrl+Shift, and drag the mouse.

▲ ▲ ▲ ▲ ▲ ▲ ▲

▼ ▼ ▼ ▼ ▼

CREATING
CHARTS AND GRAPHS

Word Graph creates bar, line, pie, and other types of charts
and inserts them into your document. You can enter data to be
charted directly in the Graph application, or copy rows and columns from a Word table.

1 Select Insert ➤ Object, and click on the Create New tab, if it
   is not already selected.

2 Select Microsoft Graph ➤ OK. The Graph window will appear with a default sample chart and data, as shown in the
   figure.

Word graph
with sample
data and graph

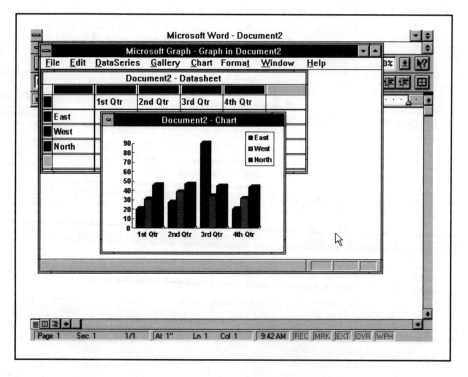

256

3 Click in the spreadsheet grid to bring into the foreground.

4 Select Edit ➤ Select All, Edit ➤ Cut, then click the mouse to deselect the table.

5 Enter the rows and columns of data you want to chart. As you enter information in the table, the graph will appear in the background window.

6 Pull down the Gallery menu and select a graph type.

7 Select File ➤ Exit and Return ➤ Yes to insert the graph in your document.

Add a frame, border, and change the size and shape of the graph as you would an imported picture. To edit the graph, double-click on it to display the Graph application.

power bar ▶ **Click graph**

Click on the Insert Chart button in the standard Toolbar to start Microsoft Graph.

tip ▶ **Instant graphs**

To chart data you've already typed in a table, select the rows and columns you want to chart, then Insert ➤ Object ➤ Microsoft Graph ➤ OK.

▲ ▲ ▲ ▲ ▲ ▲

▼ ▼ ▼ ▼ ▼

USING MICROSOFT WORDART

With Microsoft WordArt, you can create slanted, curved, filled, and rotated text for use in headlines, watermarks, eye-catching graphics, and even buttons.

1 Select Insert ➤ Object, and click on the Create New tab if it is not already selected.

2 Select Microsoft WordArt 2.0. A dialog box appears where you enter the text, and the WordArt Toolbar replaces any other Toolbars already displayed.

WordArt dialog box and Toolbar with formatted text

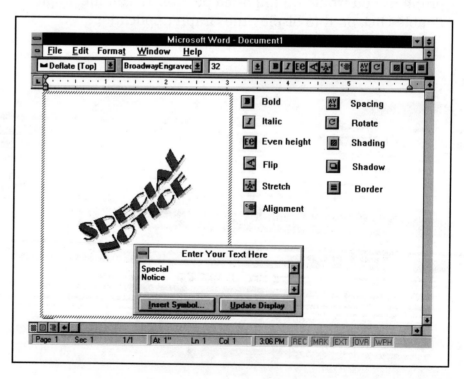

3 In the Enter Your Text Here box, type the text that you want to format using WordArt.

4 Select the shape of the text in the first list box on the Toolbar.

5 Select a font and size of the text in the next list boxes.

6 Select the special effects for the text using the remaining Toolbar buttons.

7 Click on Update Display in the dialog box to see the effects of your selections on the text.

8 To end WordArt, click in the document window. The dialog box and WordArt Toolbar disappear, and the original Toolbars reappear.

Add a frame, border, and change the size and shape of the graphic as you would an imported picture.

tip ▶ **WordArt special effects**

In addition to the list boxes for selecting the shape, font, and size of characters, the **WordArt Toolbar** contains the following buttons: *Bold* to bold all the text; *Italic* to italicize all the text; *Even Height* to make all characters the same height—regardless of case; *Flip* to rotate the text on the side; *Stretch* stretches the text vertically and horizontally; *Alignment* sets the position of the text in the graphic box; *Spacing* adjusts the amount of space between characters; *Rotate* rotates and slants the text; *Shading* displays options for fill patterns and colors; *Shadow* displays options for creating shadow characters; *Border* displays options for border thickness and style.

▲ ▲ ▲ ▲ ▲ ▲

Even the most powerful features of Word are easy. In fact, once you feel comfortable with these special Word features, you'll be creating dazzling documents!

Creating Tables

When you want to make a point with numbers, place them in a table. A table makes direct impact by letting the numbers stand out. A table draws the eye, getting immediate attention and placing the reader's focus just where you want it.

Let's create a small table now.

1 Select Table ➤ Insert Table.

2 Type **3**, then press Tab.

3 Type **4**, then select OK to display the table.

4 Press → to move to cell B1.

5 Click on the Center button (or press Ctrl+E) and type **1994**.

6 Press → to move to cell C1.

7 Click on the Center button (or press Ctrl+E) and type **1995**.

8 Move to cell A2, and type **Income**.

9 Press → and type **64,500**.

10 Press → and type **75,600**.

11 Move to cell A2, and type **Expenses**.

12 Press → and type **14,250**.

13 Press → and type **13,780**.

14 Move to cell A3, and type **Profit**. (We'll add the profit amounts later.) Check your work against Figure 4.1.

15 Select File ➤ Save.

16 Type **Profit**, then select OK.

17 Select File ➤ Exit if you are not ready to continue.

Using Formulas to Create a Spreadsheet

When we created the table named Profit, we didn't manually calculate and insert the net profit amounts. That's because we can have Word do this for us automatically by using formulas. Add the formulas now, and format the calculated cells.

1 Open PROFIT.DOC

2 Place the insertion point in cell B4.

3 Select Table ➤ Formula.

4 Press backspace to delete the text in the Formula box, except for the equal sign (=), then type **B2-B3**. It should appear like =B2-B3.

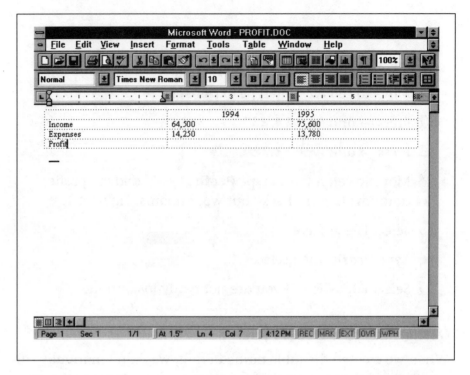

5 Select OK. The result of the calculation—50,250—appears in the cell.

6 Move to cell C4.

7 Select Table ➤ Formula.

8 Edit the Formula text box to read =C2-C3, then select OK.

Now, let's apply an automatic format to the entire table.

9 Select Table ➤ Table AutoFormat.

10 Select Classic 2, then click on OK. The table is formatted according to the selected style, as shown in Figure 4.2.

11 Select File ➤ Save.

12 Select File ➤ Print ➤ OK.

13 Select File ➤ Close.

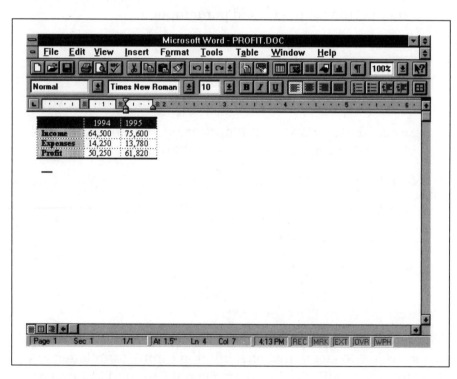

Figure 4.2:
Formatted table

Working with Columns

Now, let's see how easy it is to create newsletters. You can use any document on your disk for this exercise—you won't be saving the document in columns, just seeing how it appears.

1 Open one of your documents.

2 If your document has a title, place the insertion point in the first paragraph after the title. Otherwise, place the insertion point in front of the second paragraph.

3 Select Format ➤ Columns.

4 Select Two, the graphic representing two columns.

5 Pull down the Apply To list and select This Point Forward.

6 Select OK. Columns do not appear side-by-side in Normal view, just in Page Layout view and Print Preview.

7 Select File ➤ Print Preview.

8 Select Close.

9 Select File ➤ Close ➤ No.

10 Select File ➤ Exit if you are not ready to continue.

Creating Form Documents

Word's merge commands make it as easy to mail thousands of letters as it is to create just one. But don't think form letters are only for mass mailings. Use them even if you send just one or

two form-type letters per week, such as employment applications or requests for information.

Let's create form letters, complete with envelopes.

Constructing the Data File

The first step is to create a data file containing the variable information you want inserted into the letters. Follow these steps:

1 Select Tools ➤ Mail Merge ➤ Create ➤ Form Letters.

2 Select New Main Document.

3 Select Get Data ➤ Create Data Source.

4 In the Field Names in Headers Row, select Country.

5 Click on Remove Field Name.

6 Click on Remove Field Name twice more to delete the Home Phone and Work Phone fields.

7 Select OK to display the Save Data Source dialog box.

8 Type Maillist, then select OK.

9 Select Edit Data Source.

Next, enter the information for each copy of the form document.

10 Type **Ms.** then press Enter.

11 Type **Wilma**, then press Enter.

12 Type **Watson**, then press Enter.

13 Type **President**, then press Enter.

14 Type **Watson, Inc.**, then press Enter.

15 Type **246 Walnut St.**, then press Enter.

16 Press Enter to skip the second address line.

17 Type **Philadelphia**, then press Enter.

18 Type **PA**, then press Enter.

19 Type **19101**, then press Enter to start the second record.

20 Enter the following information for this second record, pressing Enter after each entry. When you are done, your screen should appear as in Figure 4.3.

Mr
Mark
Mellow
President
Mellow Marshmallow, Inc.
92 Park Ave.
Suite 560
New York
NY
12002

21 Select OK.

22 Select File ➤ Close ➤ Yes to save the data file.

23 Select No to not save the blank form letter.

24 Select File ➤ Exit if you're not ready to go on.

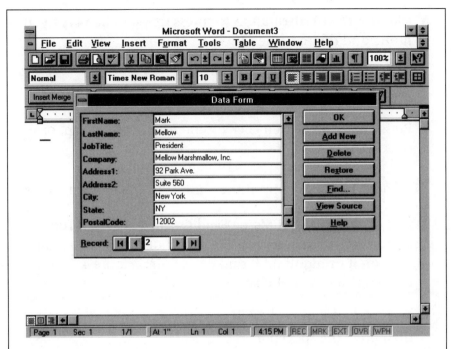

Figure 4.3:
Second record in
the data form

Writing the Form Letter

Now, write the form letter itself. Use a merge code where you want
variable information from the data file to be inserted.

1 Select Tools ➤ Mail Merge ➤ Create ➤ Form Letters.

2 Select New Main Document.

3 Select Get Data ➤ Open Data Source.

4 Double-click on MAILLIST.DOC, or select it then choose OK.

5 Select Edit Main Document.

6 Click on the Center button (or press Ctrl+E), then type your name and address, then press Enter twice.

7 Select Insert ➤ Date and Time.

8 Click on the fourth date format in the list, then select OK.

9 Press Enter twice, then click on the Align Left button, or press Ctrl+L.

Now add the codes to print the address in the merged letters.

10 Pull down the Insert Merge Field list (in the Merge Toolbar) and select Title, then press the spacebar. To select a field, click on it or highlight it and press Enter. Figure 4.4 shows the Insert Merge Field list.

11 Pull down the Insert Merge Field list and select First Name, then press the spacebar.

12 Pull down the Insert Merge Field list and select Last Name, then press Enter.

13 Pull down the Insert Merge Field list and select Job Title, then press Enter.

14 Pull down the Insert Merge Field list and select Company, then press Enter.

15 Pull down the Insert Merge Field list and select Address1, then press Enter.

16 Pull down the Insert Merge Field list and select Address2, then press Enter.

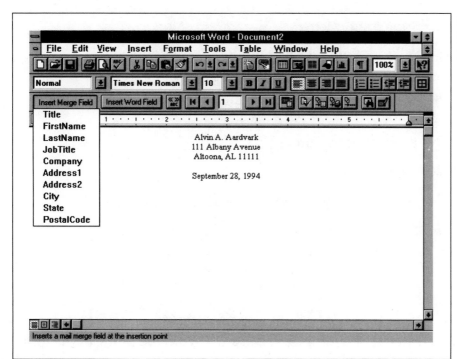

Figure 4.4:
Insert Merge
Field

17 Pull down the Insert Merge Field list and select City, then type a comma and press the spacebar.

18 Pull down the Insert Merge Field list and select State, then press the spacebar twice.

19 Pull down the Insert Merge Field list and select Postal Code, then press Enter twice.

20 Type **Dear**, then press the spacebar.

21 Pull down the Insert Merge Field list and select First Name.

22 Type the colon (:), then press Enter twice.

23 Type a short letter:

Thanks for your letter of support. I will notify you immediately after the vote is taken at the annual meeting.

Sincerely,

24 Press Enter five times.

25 Type your name.

26 Select File ➤ Save, type Support, then select OK.

27 Select File ➤ Exit if you're not ready to go on.

Compare your form letter with Figure 4.5.

Merging Form Letters and Envelopes

To generate the form letters, just tell Word the name of the form file. Do this now. But first, copy the codes that create the address so you can format and print envelopes along with the letters.

1 Open SUPPORT.DOC.

2 Select the merge codes that represent the address.

3 Select Tools ➤ Envelopes and Labels.

4 Click on the Envelopes tab. The codes for the address appear in the Delivery Address box.

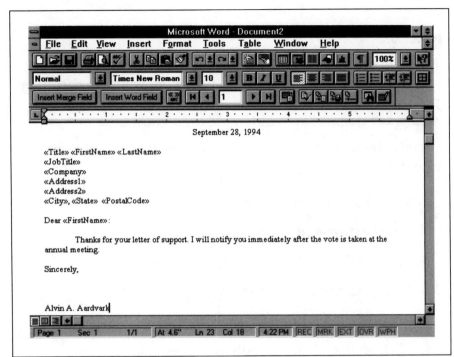

Figure 4.5:
Completed form letter

5 Select Add to Document, then No. The envelope form is added to the beginning of the form document.

6 Select Tools ➤ Mail Merge ➤ Merge ➤ Merge.

The status line will report as the letters are merged. When the process is complete, select Cancel in the Mail Merge dialog box.

7 Close all of the documents without saving them.

8 Select File ➤ Exit.

Macros

If you do much typing, you'll find yourself repeating the same series of keystrokes time and again—typing your letterhead, applying a certain format, adding page numbers or graphic elements. Create macros to automate these chores.

Let's create and use a macro that inserts your letterhead and date.

 1 Select Tools ➤ Macro ➤ Record.

 2 Type **Letterhead**, then select OK.

 3 Click on the Center button or press Ctrl+E.

 4 Type your name and address, then press Enter.

 5 Select Insert ➤ Date and Time ➤ Insert as Field ➤ OK.

 6 Click on the Align Left button or press Ctrl+L.

 7 Press Enter twice.

 8 Select Tools ➤ Macro ➤ Stop Recording to save the macro.

 9 Close the Macro dialog box, then select File ➤ Close ➤ No.

10 Click on the New button, or select File ➤ New ➤ OK. Now play the macro.

11 Select Tools ➤ Macro.

12 Double-click on Letterhead in the list box, or select Letterhead, then click on Run.

Your address appears on the screen just as you typed it.

13 Select File ➤ Close ➤ No to clear the document window.

Writing Tools

Even if you rarely use most features of Word, you'll find the speller and thesaurus to be invaluable. In fact, many writers believe they are the most useful tools that Word provides.

Speller

Get into the habit of spell-checking every document before you print it. It doesn't take very long and it can save you quite a few headaches.

Practice using the speller now. Type a short document—complete with errors—and let Word help correct it.

1 Type the following paragraphs exactly as they appear. Be sure to type in all the spelling and typographical errors.

> **Nellie Watson, former burlesq leading lady and wife of show operator and star Sliding Billy Watson, was shot and killed at at the Three Hundred Club on April 7, 1926.**

> **Mrs. Watson, who retirred from burlesque in 1918, appeared with her husband in Girls from Happyland between 1910 and 1911.**

2 Select Tools ➤ Spelling.

Word finds the first possible error and displays the dialog box shown in Figure 4.6. In this case, the name *Nellie* is not in Word's dictionary. The word will become highlighted in the text.

3 Since the word is spelled correctly, select Ignore All. The next error located is the word *Watson*.

4 Select Ignore All.

Word continues checking the document until it finds the next unknown word, *burlesq*. The correct spelling of the word is shown highlighted in the list box.

5 Double-click on the word burlesque in the list box, or select Change.
Word now detects the repetition of the word *at*.

Figure 4.6:
Spelling dialog box

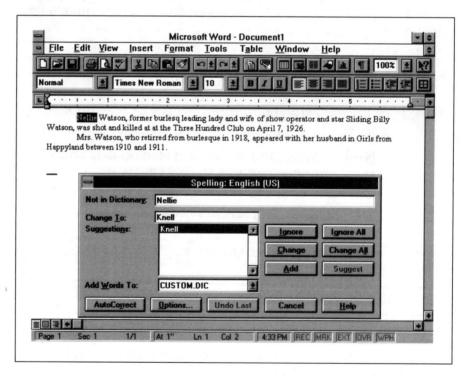

6 Select Delete to delete the duplicate word. The next word found is *retirred*.

7 Double-click on the word retired in the list box, or select Change.

Finally, Word stops at the word *Happyland*. Word can not find any alternative spellings for this word so it displays the message (no suggestions) in the suggestions list box. Let's add the word to the dictionary so it will no longer be reported as a possible error.

8 Select Add. The word will be inserted in the file CUSTOM.DIC, a supplemental dictionary file where you can store words that you want Word to accept as correct.

A box appears with the message The Spelling Check is Complete.

9 Select OK.

10 Select File ➤ Save, type **Watson**, then click on OK.

Thesaurus

Use the thesaurus when you can't think of the correct word, or when you find yourself using the same word over and over again. Just be careful. Make your selections wisely.

Let's look for a synonym for the word *former* in the document you used for the spelling check.

1 Place the insertion point anywhere in the word *former*. If you do not still have the document on the screen, just type the word **former**.

2 Select Tools ➤ Thesaurus to display the Thesaurus dialog box.

Several meanings of the word *former* are shown in the Definitions list box.

3 Click on the word onetime in the Synonyms list box, then select Replace. The word onetime replaces former in the document.

4 Select File ➤ Close ➤ No.

5 Select File ➤ Exit if you're not ready to go on.

Working with Graphics

Graphic images can add the ultimate look to your document. But as with lines and borders, don't overdo it. Avoid graphics that have no relation to the text or that will distract from your words rather than support then.

For practice, let's add a graphic image to the document Watson. We'll use DANCERS.WMF, a graphic file supplied with Word in the \CLIPART directory.

1 Open WATSON.DOC if it is not already on the screen.

2 If you are not in Page Layout view, change to it now.

3 Select Insert ➤ Picture.

4 Double-click on DANCERS.WMF, or select it then click on OK.

5 Click on the picture to select it.

6 Select Insert ➤ Frame.

7 Select Format ➤ Borders and Shading.

8 Click on the Borders tab, select Shadow, then click on OK. Your screen should appear as in Figure 4.7.

Figure 4.7:
Completed document with picture

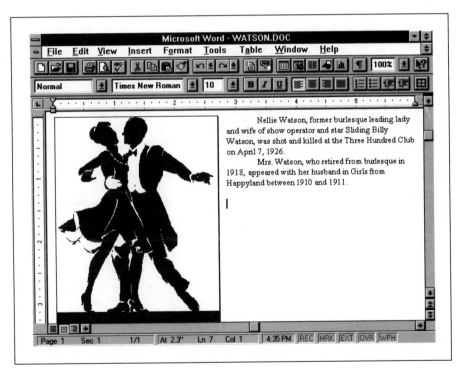

9 Select File ➤ Print ➤ OK.

10 Select File ➤ Close ➤ No.

11 Select File ➤ Exit if you are not ready to go on.

➤ ➤ ➤ ➤ ➤ ➤ ➤ ➤

▶ index

Boldface indicates primary discussions of topics.
Italic indicates illustrations.

▶ ▶ ▶ ▶ ▶ ▶ ▶

Microsoft Graph, starting, 257
Microsoft WordArt, 258–259
mouse
  copying text with, 66–67
  moving text with, **64–65**, 113
  to set margins, 169
  Shortcut menu from right mouse
    button, 69
  splitting window with, 97
moving
  graphics, 248–249
  insertion point, 44
  tab settings, 153
  toolbars, 12
  windows, 107
moving text
  with cut and paste, 68–69
  between documents, 108–109
  with mouse, **64–65**, 113
  between panes, 99
  to unopened documents, 109
multiple copies of document, print-
    ing, 26
multiple copies of text, inserting, 71
multiple documents, 95
  opening, 100–101
Multiple Pages button, on Print Pre-
    view toolbar, 25
multiple windows, displaying, 104–
    105

▶ ▶ ▶ ▶ ▶ ▶ ▶

POCKET-SIZED PC EXPERTISE.

550 pp. ISBN: 756-8.

The *PC User's es-sen'-tial, ac-ces'sible Pocket Dictionary* is the most complete, most readable computer dictionary available today. With over 2,000 plain-language entries, this inexpensive handbook offers exceptional coverage of computer industry terms at a remarkably affordable price.

In this handy reference you'll find plenty of explanatory tables and figures, practical tips, notes, and warnings, and in-depth entries on the most essential terms. You'll also appreciate the extensive cross-referencing, designed to make it easy for you to find the answers you need.

Presented in easy-to-use alphabetical order, *The PC User's es-sen'-tial, ac-ces'-si-ble Pocket Dictionary* covers every conceivable computer-related topic. Ideal for home, office, and school use, it's the only computer dictionary you need!

SYBEX. Help Yourself.

2021 Challenger Drive
Alameda, CA 94501
1-510-523-8233
1-800-227-2346

SYBEX

MAKE A GOOD COMPUTER EVEN BETTER.

350pp. ISBN: 1301-X.

The *PC Upgrade Guide for Everybody* is the no-hassle, do-it-yourself PC upgrade guide for everyone. If you know the difference between a screwdriver and a pair of pliers, this book is for you.

Inside you'll find step-by-step instructions for installing hardware to make your computer even more fun and productive. Add memory chips, CD-ROM drives and more to your PC.

You'll also learn how to diagnose minor PC problems and decide whether to repair or replace faulty components —without schlepping your PC to the shop and paying big bucks.

SYBEX. Help Yourself.

2021 Challenger Drive
Alameda, CA 94501
1-800-227-2346

SYBEX

SYBEX

FREE BROCHURE!

Complete this form today, and we'll send you a full-color brochure of Sybex bestsellers.

Please supply the name of the Sybex book purchased.

_____

How would you rate it?

_____ Excellent _____ Very Good _____ Average _____ Poor

Why did you select this particular book?

_____ Recommended to me by a friend
_____ Recommended to me by store personnel
_____ Saw an advertisement in _____
_____ Author's reputation
_____ Saw in Sybex catalog
_____ Required textbook
_____ Sybex reputation
_____ Read book review in _____
_____ In-store display
_____ Other _____

Where did you buy it?

_____ Bookstore
_____ Computer Store or Software Store
_____ Catalog (name: _____)
_____ Direct from Sybex
_____ Other: _____

Did you buy this book with your personal funds?

_____Yes _____No

About how many computer books do you buy each year?

_____ 1-3 _____ 3-5 _____ 5-7 _____ 7-9 _____ 10+

About how many Sybex books do you own?

_____ 1-3 _____ 3-5 _____ 5-7 _____ 7-9 _____ 10+

Please indicate your level of experience with the software covered in this book:

_____ Beginner _____ Intermediate _____ Advanced

Which types of software packages do you use regularly?

_____ Accounting _____ Databases _____ Networks

_____ Amiga _____ Desktop Publishing _____ Operating Systems

_____ Apple/Mac _____ File Utilities _____ Spreadsheets

_____ CAD _____ Money Management _____ Word Processing

_____ Communications _____ Languages _____ Other _____
                                                      (please specify)

Which of the following best describes your job title?

_____ Administrative/Secretarial _____ President/CEO

_____ Director _____ Manager/Supervisor

_____ Engineer/Technician _____ Other _____
(please specify)

Comments on the weaknesses/strengths of this book: _____

_____

_____

_____

_____

Name _____

Street _____

City/State/Zip _____

Phone _____

PLEASE FOLD, SEAL, AND MAIL TO SYBEX

SYBEX, INC.
Department M
2021 CHALLENGER DR.
ALAMEDA, CALIFORNIA USA
94501

SYBEX

SEAL

function	keyboard command	function	keyboard command
Lesson 9		**Lesson 11**	
Add space between paragraphs	Ctrl+0 (zero)	Page Setup	Alt+F U
Center text	Ctrl+E	**Lesson 12**	
Double spacing	Ctrl+2	AutoFormat	Ctrl+K
Justify text	Ctrl+J	Header And Footer View	Alt+Shift+R
Left-align text	Ctrl+L		
One-and-a-half spacing	Ctrl+5	Page numbers	Alt+Shift+P
Right-align text	Ctrl+R	**Lesson 13**	
Single spacing	Ctrl+1	Column break	Ctrl+Shift+Enter
Lesson 10		Select the table	Alt+5
Hanging indentation	Ctrl+T		
Indent text	Ctrl+M		
Nonbreaking hyphen	Ctrl+Shift+Hyphen		
Nonbreaking space	Ctrl+Shift+Spacebar		
Optional hyphen	Ctrl+hyphen		
Reduce hanging indentation	Ctrl+Shift+T		
Remove indentations	Ctrl+Shift+M		